MW01640297

Managing Hazardous Substances Accidents

ABOUT THE AUTHOR

Al J. Smith, Jr. has been involved with the emergency and environmental management aspects of hazardous substances spills for a dozen years. Because he has been intimately connected with more than 500 spills of oil and hazardous substances and was directly responsible for the management and mitigation of damages in several thousand spills, Mr. Smith feels that the time for developing literature and for documenting patterned response techniques is *now*.

A 1958 graduate in civil engineering from Mississippi State University (MSU) with graduate work in soil mechanics and water resources at MSU and Georgia Institute of Technology, Mr. Smith holds a Master of Science degree in environmental engineering (1970) from Vanderbilt University, a Juris Doctor (1976) from the Atlanta Law School, and a Master of Law (1980) from the Woodrow Wilson College of Law.

Mr. Smith is a contributor to the forthcoming *Toxic Substances Control Handbook* to be published by McGraw-Hill, a lecturing member of the faculty of the National Hazardous Materials Training Course, and author of numerous papers on oil and hazardous materials spills. He is a Registered Professional Engineer in four southeastern states, is certified by the National Council of State Boards of Engineering Registration, and is a member of the Georgia and American Bar Associations.

Managing Hazardous Substances Accidents

Al J. Smith, Jr.

McGraw-Hill Book Company

New York St. Louis San Francisco Auckland
Bogotá Hamburg Johannesburg London Madrid
Mexico Montreal New Delhi Panama Paris
São Paulo Singapore Sydney Tokyo Toronto

Library of Congress Cataloging in Publication Data

Smith, Al J

Managing hazardous substances accidents.

Includes index.

1. Hazardous substances—Accidents—Management.

I. Title.

T55.3.H3S64 363.1'79 80-25388

ISBN 0-07-058467-2

1234567890 KPKP 89876543210

The editors for this book were Robert Davidson and Ruth L. Weine, the designer was Mark E. Safran, and the production supervisor was Sally Fliess. It was set in Baskerville by Bi-Comp, Incorporated.

Printed and bound by The Kingsport Press

With admiration and respect, I dedicate this book to the "Father of Oil and Hazardous Spills" in this country, Kenneth E. Biglane. Without question, he has been ten years ahead of his time in this vital business. His innovative leadership inspired this book and is evident throughout the instructional content and conceptual techniques. The excellence of Ken's concepts concerning the planning for and management of spill contingencies is equaled only by that of the technology he has personally advanced.

Contents

Part Three Assistance Systems 137

Part Four Public Information 173

Preface

For years, those closest to the kinds of accidents described in this book have advanced through the school of hard knocks. Learning has come the hard way: trial and error, success and failure. But little of this information—gained at great expense to industry, government, and especially to the public and the environment—has found its way into the literature.

There is still too much confusion at the scene of the environmental accident . . . far too much overlap in applicable local, state, and federal laws. Officials complain that too many "experts," including those professing some authority but having little or none, clutter the accident scene. Many officials from outside the area burden the work force and compound the confusion by demanding to be kept informed when their need to know is in fact no greater than that of the public at large.

Individuals involved in hazardous substances accidents often do not know the extent of one another's authority and responsibilities. Most serious accidents end up gathering in more "experts" of the kind described above than actual workers, those required to clean up the scene and restore it to usefulness. This problem is largely related to a lack of training and experience as well as to too many years of ad hoc emergency response. Nor, of course, has the situation been helped by the emergence during the years 1976–1978 of new regulations at the federal level. For example, the Environmental Protection Agency (EPA) now has regulations describing "Hazardous Substances," "Toxic Emergencies," and "Hazardous Wastes." Each category was intended to be managed by a different element of EPA, though many of the various materials which can affect humans and their environment are listed in one, two, or all three of the categories. The EPA is aware of this confusion and is working to develop a coordinated agency approach.

The theory of emergency response must be based on a concept of hazardous substances accident *management.* It is not enough that we learn to secure the area, remove the injured, and finally evacuate the area; we must now ensure that the area is safe from persistent hazardous substances. Those that occupy a wreck site ten years after the accident trust us to have seen to it that the piece of land they buy is safe. They will be able to drill a well, plant a garden, and raise a family in safety because all of the possible hazards were eliminated by appropriate regulatory officials—local, state, and federal.

The purpose of this book, then, is to formulate, document, and publish a more systematic approach to the development of information, technical methodology, and field application where environmental accidents are concerned. All of the answers are not included herein; it would take a library to encompass the many aspects of this field. Moreover, the author does not possess unique knowledge and solutions. He is simply one who has been there often, taken his lumps, and made more than his share of mistakes. He hopes that others will also develop their experiences into textbook format so that the local, state, and federal officials as well as the public and industry can more effectively envision and perform their various roles. The aim of the author is to engage your interest in the total spectrum of the subject, not in just your singular responsibility (though it will remain most important to you), so that all will be truly coordinated, more knowledge-based, and more effective.

Not covered in this book are the huge disasters (floods, tornadoes, etc.) that are subject to an entirely different management scheme. The Federal Emergency Agency (FEMA) handles these events, subject to presidential declaration. Also excluded is any discussion of nuclear accidents. The Nuclear Regulatory Commission manages such events by activating the Interagency Radiological Assistance Plan (IRAP). As you read the first five chapters, you will note the author's continual reference to a lack of total jurisdiction in spill emergencies by any one governmental entity. Such was the state of the art during the 1970s and in 1980 when this text was prepared.

A helpful development is the so-called superfund legislation. This is a blanket coverage that addresses both federal jurisdiction and immediate payment of public claims for damage. The financial scheme involves participation by federal government and industry. Passage of the superfund legislation and full implementation of all its supporting regulations solves much of the jurisdictional problem by extending jurisdiction of the federal government beyond "waters of the United States." Development of this law should not substantially alter accident management concepts and basic procedures outlined in this text. Until superfund is fully implemented and properly funded, we must all be aware of and work within the system we have.

Al J. Smith

Prologue

During July 1979, State and EPA officials became aware that harmful chemicals secretly dumped into air shafts of an old coal mine were reaching the Susquehanna River near Pittston, Pennsylvania. By the middle of 1980, cleanup had cost the taxpayer $2,000,000.

At midnight, April 21, 1980, a fire erupted at a waste-disposal facility in Elizabeth, New Jersey. Some 20,000 drums of various chemicals stored there by a bankrupt company were involved in an intense fire which threatened New York City and certain heavily populated areas in New Jersey with noxious smoke from the burning toxic chemicals. By September, on-site cleanup involving such things as the recovery and processing of a huge quantity of mixed chemicals, the crushing and disposing of 7500 drums, fire control, and site stabilization had cost the State of New Jersey $8,500,000 and the Federal Government $700,000.

In Riverside County, California, from March 1980 until September, over $300,000 had been expended cleaning up what is being called the "Stringfellow Hazardous Waste Site."

At Muldraugh, Kentucky, July 26, 1980, a train derailment involved burning vinyl chloride and the evacuation of 2500 persons. A prediction of lengthy evacuation and the fear of a BLEVE (boiling liquid expanding vapor explosion) caused state and federal agents in concert with railroad officials to use explosive devices in order to vent and accelerate the burning of the chemical.

We recall the traumas at Molino, Florida and Seymour, Indiana . . . the burning of pesticide warehouses in Texas, Tennessee, and Florida. In fact, these events are relatively easy to remember, even for those not involved in any way. What most of us can't recall is how the event was responded to and managed. It is true that we occasionally read a critical report written by some peripheral official or observer, but do we really know what happened? Was government and industry response ad hoc, or was the response a result of preplanning and consequently a reasonably well-articulated happening? The answers to these questions are the basic fiber of this text.

Without question, there is a basic nucleus of accident management alive and well in the United States, and, despite our growing public concern with hazardous substances spills and uncontrolled hazardous waste sites, our national ability to cope has existed in the form of a National Contingency Plan since 1968. Our problem lies in pulling together what we have and ensuring that we don't become diffuse. As we look down the road into the 1980s, we must not reinvent the wheel; we must solidify and amplify our current concepts and technical tools. The concern here is that the public clamor and technical appeal involved with hazardous spills and waste site pursuits could cause regulators to lose perspective.

ACKNOWLEDGMENTS

The illustrations and text content of this book have been used to make a point, forward a method, or issue a caution. It is not the author's intent to identify any person, company, or government in an embarrassing light.

The author writes this book in his private capacity; the views are his own and are based on his experiences combined with the information freely contributed by so many of you out there who perform daily with willingness and courage. Therefore, the author thanks all of you who work with the sheriff's office, the city council, civil defense organization, fire department, state highway patrol, Salvation Army, Red Cross, and state and federal agencies . . . and who collectively are the authors of this book.

Finally, sincere thanks to the U.S. Environmental Protection Agency, the U.S. Coast Guard, the National Oceanographic and Atmospheric Administration, and to the other groups mentioned in the text for the use of the illustrations discussed above.

Managing Hazardous Substances Accidents

part ONE

Management

chapter
ONE

Laws and Levels of Interest

1-1 BACKGROUND

What have we been doing about hazardous substance spills over the past 100 years? The truth is, not much until the middle sixties. Up until that time, a showing of actual deaths or diseases resulting from a specific event was necessary to motivate serious federal response. In 1965 Congress took the initiative for change, declaring that environmental degradation and contamination no longer needed to be quantified in terms of disease and death in order to be recognized as a national problem.

From the U.S. Public Health Service, the federal government in 1966 formed a separate agency with new ideas, new parameters, and new goals: the Federal Water Pollution Control Administration. Later renamed the Federal Water Quality Administration, this agency was placed in the Department of the Interior. In 1970 the agency was augmented with air, solid waste, and pesticide jurisdictions and was renamed the Environmental Protection Agency (EPA).

During this evolution, the basic water law (Public Law 92-500, the Federal Water Pollution Control Act) was amended a number of times. One of the most important of these amendments was Section 311, Oil and Hazardous Substance Spills—the first significant mention of hazardous spills to appear in federal law. Inserted in 1970, Section 311 generally addressed pollution problems in waters of the United States. Under this amendment, EPA and the U.S. Coast Guard were mandated to regulate (by prevention and/or enforcement) spills of oil and/or hazardous substances. The President's Council on Environmental Quality was directed to develop a national contingency plan for the coordinated, prompt, and comprehensive response to these spills. This plan, one of the most significant documents in the field of hazardous spills, will be discussed in detail throughout this book and referred to as the 1510 plan.

In 1972 and 1977, the Congress made Section 311 more specific. The 1977 amendment was designed to support the development of specific and enforceable hazardous substance spill regulations, which would complement already well-developed oil spill regulations.

In the meantime, public interest in environmental emergencies had steadily increased. While water-related accidents had pervaded the field, air episodes moved into an equal position of concern. A rash of train accidents in 1977, 1978, 1979, and 1980 actually raised a national public outcry for regulation and refocused regulators' attention on public protection. Back-to-back events, such as train wrecks at Pensacola, Florida (anhydrous ammonia), Waverly, Tennessee (LPG), Leon, Kentucky (acrylonitrile), and Youngstown, Florida (chlorine), which killed dozens, injured hundreds, and closed public water supplies, stimulated a national reaction to environmental emergencies.

In response to these outcries and supported by the 1977 amendment to Section 311, the Environmental Protection Agency promulgated hazardous substance spill regulations in 1978. Revised and published in August of 1979, they basically provide for:

1 A civil fine up to $250,000 for the spill

2 A criminal sanction (fine and jail term) for spillors* that fail to immediately report the accident to the appropriate federal agency

3 Access to the "Section K" contingency fund when the spillor is unknown or cannot or will not clean up

4 The restraint of spilling through court order when actual or potential threats to public health and welfare are obvious

5 Regulation of industry for the prevention of spills as well as for spill response

The problem has been and continues to be one of defining what chemicals are *hazardous* when spilled, and in what quantities they must be spilled to be *harmful* to U.S. waters, to the environment, and to public health and welfare.

As federal regulations were being developed, state governments began to reinforce their regulations and develop new ones. Local agencies (civil defense, fire departments, and volunteer groups) began to be more directly involved in aspects of accidents other than life or limb protection, as well as in accident prevention. In Selma, Alabama, local law enforcement officials actually restrained train traffic until poorly maintained rails were repaired. In Atlanta, Georgia, all truck traffic was prohibited from entering the city beginning December 1, 1978, unless licensed to unload therein; dangerous cargoes

* The word *spillor* is used in this book to designate the entity responsible for a spill and for initiating and funding the subsequent cleanup.

were one factor in this decision. In early 1978, the governor of Kentucky was so concerned with the number of train derailments in his state that he called the railroad companies in and asked them to explain what they were going to do to control this expanding problem.

The transportation industry is working to improve the system. Railroads are repairing and improving their tracks; the trucking and pipeline industries are improving their physical stock; fixed facilities are developing contingency plans. The chemical industry continues to grow, however, and with this growth the need for transportation expands. The railroad companies are required by federal law to haul hazardous cargo. The public demands it. When you brush your teeth, develop your film, or type a letter, you increase the need for the manufacture and transportation of chemicals.

This is the way we live, but we must not let our actions be unguided *reactions.* We must look at past experiences and train ourselves to prevent accidents as far as possible and to respond to them adequately when they occur. This can only be done through training, which can only be achieved through well-documented text materials.

1-2 SCOPE AND DEFINITIONS

Because hazardous substance accidents more frequently occur inland of the coastline, we will be discussing only inland situations and the laws applicable to them. Since the literature on the harmful effects of chemical and oil spills is plentiful, the *need* for damage mitigation and cleanup is not an issue in this text. The presumption is that when there is a spill, there will be some form of government response, containment, mitigation, and cleanup.

The word *accident* is used to refer to spills of materials that can be directly harmful to human life or damaging to its supporting environment. A *spill* may be a burning pesticide warehouse being washed down with fire hoses; a truck or train wreck releasing hazardous chemicals into the air or the surrounding land or water; a sinking boat loaded with fuel or other cargo; or, finally, a potential tank rupture creating an imminent and substantial threat to human life and its environment.

Terms will be a problem for the reader, but they must be grasped; trade talk is being used in spill events on an international basis. *RRT* (regional response team, *NRT* (national response team), *OSC* (on-scene coordinator), and the *1510 plan* typify this growing language, and while initially it is mind-boggling, experience and study will gradually diminish the confusion.

1-3 FEDERAL LAWS AND LEVELS OF INTEREST

Just one 1976 publication listing the various laws and regulations dealing with the environment weighs about a pound. You may never need to know about many of these laws and regulations, but you may well be interested in a list of federal laws that bear on accidents involving hazardous substances.

When they are not out of print, the following may be ordered by name by telephoning the inquiry desk of the U.S. Government Printing Office at (202) 783-3238:

1 The Federal Water Pollution Control Act of 1978, with these supporting regulations. Pay special attention to Section 311 in the Act:
- **(a)** 40 CFR, Part 112: Oil Spill Prevention
- **(b)** 40 CFR, Parts 116 and 117: Hazardous Substances
- **(c)** 40 CFR, Part 1510: National Oil and Hazardous Substances Pollution Contingency Plan
- **(d)** 40 CFR, Part 151: Hazardous Substances Spill Prevention
- **(e)** 40 CFR, Part 110: Harmful Discharge of Oil
- **(f)** 33 CFR, Parts 151–156: Oil Spills and Prevention
- **(g)** 40 CFR, Part 109: State Contingency Plan Criteria

2 Ports and Waterway Safety Act, with supporting regulations:
- **(a)** 33 CFR, Part 124: Waterfront Safety
- **(b)** 33 CFR, Parts 125 and 126: Waterfront Security Zones and Regulated Navigable Areas

3 49 CFR, Parts 171–176: Hazardous Material Transportation Regulations
4 Rivers and Harbors Act
5 Federal Insecticide, Fungicide, and Rodenticide Act
6 Toxic Substances Control Act (TSCA)
7 Resource Conservation and Recovery Act (RCRA)
8 Clean Air Act
9 Marine Protection, Research, and Sanctuaries Act
10 Intervention on High Seas Act
11 Disaster Relief Act
12 Public Law 9-20, The Federal Civil Defense Act

Of course, this only briefly outlines the federal interests in hazardous substances accidents. Many laws and regulations are not listed, but you can see that the problem is complex.

Under Public Law 92-500, Section 311, the federal government is automatically involved when spills of oil or hazardous substances threaten waters of the United States. There are also two other levels of government involved. Even considering statutory preemption and federal primacy arguments, there will always be the need for state and local governmental participation. Thus whenever hazardous substances threaten waters of the United States, anyone exercising individual authority must take care to recognize these various jurisdictions. Obviously, many authorities may overlap or conflict. In addition, most accidents will require assessment and decisions, and many voices must be heard before the wisest resolution is established. There will be proprietary feelings; unyielding prerogatives; safety, health, and environmental issues;

law-enforcement issues; and yes, even politics, but the principal issue will always be *protection of the public welfare, which is, or could be, affected.*

We have now identified a minimum base of three levels of government, mentioned a few of the laws that will motivate the federal sector, and recognized the potential confusion of authorities and activities in a spill response. One can imagine the nightmare associated with a hazardous substance accident which has no one in charge, or perhaps five or ten people in charge. The question will also arise: How can *one* person be in total charge? Examine the responsibilities, consider the issues, and review the laws; there is no way this will ever be practical if the phrase *in charge* is strictly defined. One thing is certain, however: Someone or something must ultimately *manage* the operation. What then is a practical and sane management scheme for these traumatic events?

Item 1(c) on the list of federal laws in this chapter, the National Oil and Hazardous Substances Pollution Contingency Plan (40 CFR, Part 1510), is at present the federal document that best responds to this need. Published and updated by the Council on Environmental Quality (CEQ), this plan, referred to in this book as the 1510 plan, outlines a complete scenario of spill response. It also provides a forum for the participation of all levels of government and other interests by establishing regional response teams (RRT), to be discussed in the next chapters. This national plan, along with the EPA and/or U.S. Coast Guard regional plans, are documents you must get and read. They should be readily available to you through the nearest Coast Guard district office and the appropriate EPA regional headquarters. Also, the state civil defense office together with the state pollution control authority should supply copies of any state-level contingency plans for hazardous-substance accidents. The local civil defense director is in the best position to know of local contingency plans. After you have carefully reviewed all this material, you will still be confused, but one clear concept will begin to come through—that of a *coordinated team.* There is within each federal EPA region and Coast Guard district, a full-time oil and hazardous substance spill program. In each of the 10 EPA regional offices, the emergency group (usually referred to as the Environmental Emergency Branch) is charged with the implementation of the inland portion of the spill law. Each of the 12 Coast Guard district offices has a similar operation for coastal waters. While reasonably uniform in the Coast Guard, these programs have varied substantially from one EPA region to another. At this writing, and as a result of in-depth studies, EPA is making a national effort to beef up its emergency forces and hopes to equalize the intensity of activity in all 10 EPA regions.

Available on 24-hour alert to supplement these field teams are three trained and equipped Coast Guard *strike teams,* located on the East, West, and Gulf Coasts, and an EPA *emergency response team* (ERT). See Figures 1-1 to 1-3. These will be described more fully in Chapter 3.

A regional contingency plan is drawn up by each of these EPA and Coast Guard groups and used as a principal functional document. Each plan com-

Fig. 1-1 A regional EPA Emergency Response Team.

prises both the 1510 national contingency plan and a regional amplification of it. The two together form the only *detailed,* tried and proven federal emergency coordination plan for hazardous substance spills in operation in the United States today. Containing instructions for every aspect of a spill situation, this plan is, as previously mentioned, a must for anyone who has even a remote responsibility associated with spills. Whether you are a firefighter, police officer, civil defense worker, etc., or the unfortunate spillor, you can read the 1510 plan (referring now to the *combined* national and regional contingency plan for your area) and get a feeling about where you fit in the federal scheme.

No planning document is perfect, and, of course, this one isn't either. The

Fig. 1-2 The command post of a U.S. Coast Guard strike team on scene at Crestview, Florida, April 1979.

Fig. 1-3 U.S. Coast Guard strike team members on scene at Crestview, Florida.

limitations involve scope, however, not workability; i.e., the 1510 plan only covers spills which threaten *waters* of the United States. This means that unless a body of water is clearly involved in a hazardous substance spill, federal jurisdiction in terms of Section 311 is questionable. The confusion that has evolved among officials at recent accidents across the country is related directly to the fact that there is no national master plan covering *all* types of emergencies.

Perhaps several case histories will help identify the limitations mentioned above.

LEON, KENTUCKY, JANUARY **1978:** Here a train derailment caused the spillage of acrylonitrile into the local stream system, and resulted in shutting off the water supplies of two towns. The chemical had to be purged from the ground before the stream residuals were brought down to acceptable levels for drinking water. Because a body of water was clearly involved, the on-scene scenario was controlled by the 1510 plan. Let's call this a type I emergency—one in which the 1510 national and regional contingency plans control the total response effort.

YOUNGSTOWN, FLORIDA, FEBRUARY **1978:** Another train derailment, with chlorine as the key chemical spilled, occurred north of Panama City in the community of Youngstown. Eight people were killed. Continual spillage of chlorine and a leaking car of liquid propane gas (LPG) necessitated the evacuation of several thousand people. The 1510 plan was used initially as a coordinating document because of the seriousness of the event and the possible involvement of water. But because the threat to water systems was difficult to prove, the jurisdiction of 1510 was questionable, and the plan did not remain in effect throughout the entire accident. Thus the on-scene scenario was not as clearly regulated as in the Leon, Kentucky, situation because waters of the United States were not clearly affected. This we will call a type II emergency—one that involves a gray area.

WAVERLY, TENNESSEE, FEBRUARY **1978:** Once again a train derailment involving liquid propane gas created an emergency situation. In this case, an explosion during rerailing killed a number of people. Since there was clearly no threat to any body of water, the 1510 plan was not involved. This we will call a type III emergency.

The 1510 plan works where it is appropriately used; there is no question about that. Twelve years of experience document its success story. The problem is that it doesn't go far enough. Unless there is a body of water nearby, the public is not protected. And, like any other plan, the 1510 plan begins to break down if it is used beyond its intent. There is no doubt, however, that this plan could serve as a nucleus on which to build a national contingency plan for all emergencies. Chapter 2 contains much more discussion about the dynamics of the 1510 plan. Now, however, let's discuss the other levels of government and their concerns with hazardous substance accident planning.

1-4 STATE GOVERNMENT: LAWS AND ORGANIZATIONS

A review of each state's position on hazardous substances accident response could—in fact, does—fill a book. During the period 1977–1978, under contract to a special EPA task force, the Arthur D. Little Company studied in depth the environmental response capabilities of 11 states: Arkansas, California, Colorado, Connecticut, Indiana, Kentucky, Louisiana, Mississippi, New Jersey, Ohio, and Pennsylvania—a good cross section. This 2-year study revealed a number of interesting things.

This writer (an original task force member) has done a similar but simplified study of the eight Southeastern states. With a clear understanding that to generalize is to err, we can make some general inferences from these studies.

Laws

1 Most states lack direct statutory authority concerning hazardous substance spills. Pollution is usually considered a misdemeanor rather than a violation of specific statutes with specific penalties.

2 Public health laws are generally not broad enough to be of direct use in spill emergencies.

3 Use of the term *man-made emergencies* in state law limits the emergency response powers in about half the states.

4 Fish and game laws speak more to the collection of funds for damages caused to wildlife than to cleanup or enforcement concepts.

5 Local covenants (zoning, etc.) can be helpful in specific cases but are not really broad enough to cover the mitigation phase of an accident.

6 Research shows that where state government is concerned, specific pollution statutes (dealing with air and water) are the most precise authority and effective guidelines for dealing with emergencies caused by hazardous substances.

Organizations

A growing number of states are moving toward the concept that the governor's coordinating official will be the staff civil defense director. This person or office will coordinate the state response to an emergency by forming a state response team appropriately patterned to fit the character of the accident (oil, hazardous substances, fire, flood). There are hardly more than 20 states with a predesignated state on-scene coordinator (OSC) and only 10 of these have full-time spill response personnel that are educated, trained, and skilled in the field of hazardous substances. Every state has some form of disaster response capability and an ongoing public health program (Figure 1-4). Most states have a fish and wildlife statute and regulating body, and, of course, an air and water pollution authority.

Historically, the air and water pollution control authority in each state has been closely tied to the 1510 plan. In 1977 a majority of governors named this state agency to sit on the regional response team (RRT). Recently, however, several governors have appointed their civil defense organizations to serve in this capacity. In the past, states were only unofficial members of the RRT; in 1980 they were made official, primary members under the national contingency plan. The significance of this membership will become clear as we move along, but for now try to envision it as a rather unique merger of federal and state interests.

Fig. 1-4 A North Carolina state cooperative deploys equipment.

Despite the wide diversity of their resources, expertise, organization, and laws, all the states, without exception, assert a keen interest in actively participating in hazardous substance accidents.

1-5 LOCAL GOVERNMENT: LAWS AND ORGANIZATIONS

Laws

When there is an accident involving a hazardous substance, no one is more involved than the local authorities. Law at the local level is generally described as police power emanating from local codes and ordinances, with some authority extending from the state constitution. As for authority to regulate any cleanup beyond the initial emergency (fire, evacuation), the local entities have little or none.

In terms of prevention, the local entities are beginning to flex more muscle. Restrictive zoning for industries in the hazardous substance business is today a growing reality. Some cities are getting involved (via police powers) in regulating transportation through their incorporated areas, and there is evidence that state government is helping cities regulate beyond their city limits. As mentioned earlier, police authorities in Selma, Alabama, restrained train traffic until rails were repaired. Trucks cannot enter the Interstate I-285 perimeter surrounding Atlanta without a permit showing their business is actually in Atlanta.

Organizations

Having been at the accident first, having fearlessly confronted the initial dangers, tended to the dead or injured, and evacuated the area, the local officials and volunteers suddenly discover (somewhere from 2 to 6 hours after impact) that a legion of outsiders has descended upon them. In the face of this invasion, terror gives way to confusion, which can, and on occasion does, become anger and resentment. When all the invading officials (federal and state alike) have satisfied themselves that the job is done and have left the scene, there remains once again the group of local people to contend with the results—good or bad.

At Crestview, Florida, during the April 1979 train accident, there were over 150 officials present, each acting in some government capacity (Figure 1-5). There were 18 "visiting" officials from out of state who wanted to "observe," and 20 media representatives. Moreover, at the peak of cleanup, there were only 23 actual workers handling all moving of cars, patching of leaks, and rerailing. This is becoming typical of the serious accident scene, and as interest continues to grow, the number of officials in attendance will increase accordingly. Curiosity, "the mother of danger," is rampant at every

Fig. 1-5 A huddle of officials involved in the derailment at Crestview, Florida, April 1979.

one of these events. Well-meaning, nonofficial onlookers also want to know and want to help, but they are nonetheless part of the problem by their very presence. Like the various officials, they must be managed. It is the management of all these people, as well as the media, in tight quarters and under circumstances of extreme stress that measures the success of the response operation in terms of those locally involved. The sheriff's department, fire department, local police, civil defense organization, highway patrol, National Guard (included here because its role is local in effect), and the county judge—all must coordinate their actions to ensure that on-scene order is maintained.

Enough cannot be said about the special aid groups: the Salvation Army, the American Red Cross, the emergency medical teams (EMT), the local hospitals, and the local volunteer groups that are so involved in the sociological aspects of the accident. It is not commonly known that on a national basis the civil defense organization (by agreement) coordinates the Red Cross and the Salvation Army to avoid duplication of effort. The civil defense organization, in fact, coordinates many on-scene services that go largely unnoticed but are absolutely vital. It is the author's opinion that the two most vital on-scene coordinators are the federal OSC and the civil defense official. Usually, there are three civil defense representatives involved in an incident: the local director, a state coordinator, and a FEMA (Federal Emergency Management Agency) representative. The FEMA representative and either the state or local coordinator (depending on availability) should serve on the RRT and *must* keep all local officials advised.

1-6 INDUSTRY

Section 311 stipulates that in a spill emergency the spillor must be given an opportunity to clean up and mitigate harm from its own accident. As backup, a multimillion dollar emergency fund is available to the federal OSC, who is to immediately perform this duty should the spillor fail. This fund is managed by the Coast Guard and available 24 hours a day, 7 days a week. As a practical matter, the OSC must judge, with the help of the regional response team (check it out; you may be a member), whether or not the accident cleanup is progressing properly. The RRT's assessment will help the OSC decide not only the cleanup priorities but also whether or not federal money is necessary to augment or supplant industry's effort.

Industry, which is usually *but not always* the spillor (federal, local, and state entities can spill too), responded to the Arthur D. Little survey by saying that it desires to clean up its spills. A 12-year track record indicates that this is generally true. Although an argument could develop over the degree and quality of unregulated cleanup in the past, it is only fair to say that, with exceptions (the *60 Minutes* variety), industry has been cleaning up accidents to some degree for years without any direct federal, state, or local statutory sanctions. Industry is quite sensitive about its public image, and in about 70 percent of all spills either performs the cleanup or contracts it out. Some industries maintain their own chemical and oil expertise groups through cooperatives. A number of oil spill contractors have also appeared throughout the country, and over the past 11 years some rather exotic oil spill cleanup and recovery equipment has been developed. The hazardous substance contractor and specialized cleanup tools, however, are at this writing rare breeds.

There is clearly a fast-growing need for competent, well-trained, educated, and experienced hazardous substance cleanup contractors. Like the oil spill cleanup industry, they must be ready to respond at a moment's notice. There is as much difference, however, between the response to an oil spill and a hazardous substance spill as there is between night and day. There will be far more credential checking in the hazardous substance business. The liability of industry must be minimized, and the public cannot—must not—be subjected to inadequately trained people servicing a cleanup operation.

Let's dwell on this a moment. At a recent accident involving a number of chemicals, air-monitoring equipment detected three distinct toxic gases: chlorine, phosgene, and ammonia. There was also a mixture of toxic liquid compounds: carbon tetrachloride, phenol, and others—a real boilermaker. The ground was soaked, the river was moderately polluted, and the air was contaminated for miles. One car of anhydrous ammonia had exploded, leaving the two halves of the tank car 1600 feet (488 m) apart. The only things missing were a few cars of leaking liquid propane gas and perhaps some aminotoluene or acrylonitrile. Can you just imagine the scope of this? Should you use conventional, well-trained oil spill cleanup crews, or transient labor? Is it enough to rerail the cars, skim the pollutant, and patch the ruptured cars? Is it enough to contain and remove the contaminated soil and design a turbidity screen for the river? Do we put out the fire, thus spreading the unquantified and unknown mixed chemicals with water, or do we let the burning car burn? Can we advance the burning by explosive techniques? Do we dump the chlorine car? Remember, while we contemplate, people are out of their homes.

Fig. 1-6 A specialized rerailing crew at work.

During an event such as described above, and as seen in Figures 1-6 through 1-13, there may be need for a half-dozen cleanup specialists in the hazardous substance accident. You can see why industry has not developed complete response capability, in spite of the motivating factors of reputation, professional pride, and costs.

Fig. 1-7 An expert hazardous substance cleanup crew at work.

Fig. 1-8 A specialized chemical team involved in cleanup.

Fig. 1-9 A cleanup crew using specialized cleanup equipment.

Fig. 1-10 A track-repair crew.

Fig. 1-11 Washing chemicals into a collection basin for disposal.

Fig. 1-12 Redrumming dangerous chemicals after a 1978 flood of the Ohio River spread drums (some leaking) across the countryside near Shepherdsville, Kentucky.

Fig. 1-13 A vital part of cleanup may be an improvised treatment system for surface drainage water mixed with chemicals.

chapter
TWO
Contingency Planning

In Chapter 1 we talked briefly about the interrelationship of laws, contingency plans, and levels of interest in the field of hazardous spills. Now we will take a closer look at contingency planning, including those areas for which plans still do not exist, and make some suggestions for the present and future.

2-1 THE NATIONAL OIL AND HAZARDOUS SUBSTANCES POLLUTION CONTINGENCY PLAN (1510 PLAN)

This writer has been involved with the 1510 plan as a guide for spill response in the eight Southeastern states for 12 years and can say without reservation that no other federal document has made more sense. Once again you are exhorted to get one and read it if you haven't already done so. No one is eager to read a federal regulation, but this one is worth your while and will take no more than an hour. It is without question the only current planning document codified as federal law that reflects the aforementioned coordinated team concept. The 1510 plan outlines a complete scenario of spill response. It provides a forum—*the only forum* at the scene—known as the regional response team (RRT) which encourages, even insists on the full participation of federal, state, and local government. The plan predesignates a presiding officer and lists the various agencies with legal authority to participate as members of this team. It identifies an on-scene coordinator (OSC) at the federal level and outlines basic ground rules for the mitigation of damage from the spill.

The 1510 plan also provides for a National Response Team (NRT) which meets regularly in Washington. This group provides national policy guidance and works continually with the Council on Environmental Quality (CEQ) in updating the plan. The NRT monitors significant accidents involving spills of oil and hazardous substances and can, on request of the RRT, resolve major issues. Should an event become so large or so sociologically or technically involved as to outstrip the RRT's capabilities, the NRT could become actively involved. The NRT is chaired by EPA. Its members are high-level officials of the following federal agencies: EPA, the Department of Transportation (DOT) represented by the U.S. Coast Guard, Department of Defense (DOD), Department of Commerce (DOC) represented by the National Oceanographic and Atmospheric Administration (NOAA), the Federal Emergency Management Agency (FEMA), the Department of Agriculture (USDA), Department of Justice (DOJ), Department of Health and Human Services (HHS), Department of Labor (DOL), Department of Energy (DOE), Department of State (DOS), and the Department of Interior (DOI). The National Transportation and Safety Board (NTSB) is a liaison member. Members are added as national interests change in the hazardous accident business.

Before going forward, some definitions and descriptions are in order to clarify and expand what has been said about the plan. These are quoted directly from selected portions of 40 CFR, Part 1510.

§1510.3 Scope

(a) The Plan applies to all Federal agencies and is in effect for the navigable waters of the United States and adjoining shorelines, for the contiguous zone, and the high seas beyond the contiguous zone in connection with activities under the Outer Continental Shelf Lands Act or the Deep Water Port Act of 1974, or which may affect natural resources belonging to, appertaining to, or under the exclusive management authority of the United States (including resources under the Fishery Conservation and Management Act of 1976), (See Sections 311(b)(1) and 502(7) of the Clean Water Act).

(b) Implementation of this Plan is complementary to the Joint U.S./Canadian Contingency Plan (including the annexes pertaining to the Great Lakes, and the Eastern and Western coastal areas); the Joint U.S./Mexican Contingency Plan (when adopted by both parties); and international assistance plans and agreements, security regulations, and responsibilities based upon Federal statutes and Executive Orders. This Plan shall be utilized to coordinate U.S. involvement in pollution incidents occurring in waters not under the management jurisdiction of the United States.

§1510.5(k) The On-Scene Coordinator

On-Scene Coordinator (OSC) means the Federal official predesignated by the EPA or the USCG to coordinate and direct the Federal response to spills, and discharge removal efforts at the scene of a discharge.

§1510.21 Federal Responsibility

(a) This Plan seeks to insure a coordinated Federal response at the scene of a discharge of oil or hazardous substance that poses a threat to the public health or welfare. In the event of a discharge, the Federal OSC shall first promptly determine (under Section 311(c)(1) of the Act) whether the person responsible for the discharge is taking proper action to remove the discharge or threat of discharge. If practicable, the OSC shall make the person responsible aware of his financial responsibility. If the OSC determines that the person responsible is taking proper action, the OSC shall monitor progress and provide advice. If the person responsible does not act promptly or fails to take proper removal actions, or if the person responsible is unknown, or if a potential discharge is considered to exist, further Federal response actions shall be undertaken promptly in accordance with this Plan.

§1510.31 Emergency Response Activities and Coordination

(a) In a pollution emergency, the OSC is responsible for Federal on-scene coordination. The OSC provides reports to and receives advice from the RRT charged with regional coordination. The RRT is composed of representatives from the regional and district offices of the participating agencies, States, and local governments.

§1510.34 Regional Response Team

(a) The RRT serves as the regional body for planning and preparedness actions before a pollution discharge and for coordination and advice during a pollution discharge. The RRT consists of regional representatives of the participating agencies, state, and local government representatives as appropriate.

§1510.23 Non-Federal Participation

(a) Every State Governor is asked to assign an office or agency to represent the State on the RRT. The State's representative should participate fully in all facets of RRT activities and shall designate the element of the State government that will direct state supervised discharge removal operations. Participation of officials from municipalities with major ports and waterways is also invited in the RRT. [See §1510.34(f).]

State and local government agencies are encouraged to include contingency planning for discharge removal in all emergency and disaster planning. Federal local contingency plans required by this Plan shall be coordinated with plans developed by state and local governments. This is especially important for traffic control, land access, and disposal of pollutants in removal operations.

(b) States, industry groups, academic organizations, and others are encouraged to commit resources for removal operations. Specific commitments shall be listed in Federal regional and local contingency plans. EPA and the USCG should explore the possibility of concluding memoranda delegating responsibility to concerned States for cleanup of certain spills. Details on reimbursement to states for removal actions taken under to this Plan are contained in §1510.65 and 33 CFR Part 153.

§1510.63 General Pattern of Response Actions

(a) When the OSC receives a report of a discharge or potential discharge, he should normally take action in the following sequence:

(1) Investigate the report to determine pertinent information such as the threat posed to public health or welfare, the type and quantity of material discharged, and the source of the discharge.

(2) Notify RRT members and the Scientific Support Coordinator, in accordance with the applicable regional plan.

(3) Determine, in accordance with Section 311(c)(1) of the Act, whether the discharger (that is, the owner or operator of the vessel, onshore facility, or offshore facility from which the discharge occurs) is properly carrying out removal actions. Removal is being done properly when:

(*i*) The discharger's cleanup is fully sufficient to minimize or mitigate damage to the public welfare. The discharger's removal efforts are "improper" to the extent that Federal efforts are necessary to prevent further damage; and

(*ii*) The discharger's removal efforts are in accordance with applicable regulations and guidelines, including this Plan, especially Annex X.

(4) Officially classify the severity of the discharge and determine the course of action to be followed.

(5) Determine whether state action to effect removal is necessary within the meaning of Section 311(c)(2)(H) of the Act (See §1510.65(h)).

(b) The preliminary inquiry will probably show that the situation falls into one of five classes. [Three of] These classes and the appropriate response to each are outlined below:

(1) If the investigation shows that the initial information overstated the magnitude or danger of the discharge and no environmental pollution or potential pollution is involved, the case shall be considered a false alarm and should be closed.

(2) If the investigation shows a minor discharge with the discharger taking appropriate removal action, contact should be established with the discharger. The removal action should be monitored to insure continued proper action by the discharger.

(3) If the investigation shows a minor discharge with improper removal action being taken, the following measures shall be taken:

(*i*) An immediate effort should be made to prevent further discharges from the source.

(*ii*) The discharger shall be advised of the proper action to be taken.

(*iii*) If the discharger does not follow this advice, warning of the discharger's liability for the cost of removal, pursuant to §311(f) of the Act, shall be given.

§1510.37 Public Information Network

(a)(1) When a major pollution incident occurs, it is imperative to give the public prompt, accurate information on the nature of the discharge and actions underway to mitigate the damage. . . . Prompt disclosure of the facts helps to encourage cooperation by interested parties and to check the spread of misinformation. National administration policy and the Freedom of Information Act both call for maximum disclosure of information.

(c) An on-scene news office will be established upon the request of any agency participating on the RRT or the OSC to coordinate media relations and issue official Federal information on a pollution incident. The office will be staffed according to regional plans and applicable agency directives. Whenever possible, the on-scene news office will be headed by a representative of the agency providing the OSC. Any participating agency may, by request to the RRT, place a representative on the staff of the news office. The OSC shall determine location of the on-scene news office but every effort should be made to locate it near the scene of the pollution incident.

(1) The director of the on-scene news office shall coordinate all public information activities for the OSC. . . .

§1510.65 Funding

(a) If the person responsible for the discharge or threat of discharge does not act promptly, or take proper removal actions, or if the person responsible for the discharge is unknown, Federal discharge removal actions may begin under Section 311(c)(1) of the Act.

§1510.57 Special Considerations

(a) *Safety of personnel.*—Actual or potential polluting discharges threatening damage to air and water can also threaten human health and safety. The OSC should be aware of the hazards, should exercise great caution in allowing civilian or government personnel into the affected area until the nature of the substance discharged is known, and due caution should be exercised thereafter. Local contingency plans shall identify sources of information on anticipated hazards, precautions, and requirements to protect personnel during response operations. Names and phone numbers of people with relevant information shall be included.

These brief notations are taken from the latest edition of the National Oil and Hazardous Substances Pollution Contingency Plan. Some statements are not complete; therefore it is necessary to study the entire document in order to fully understand how the system works. Even from this brief extract, however, you can see that the plan has considerable merit. Figures 2-1 through 2-3 graphically describe some of the organizational functions of federal contingency planning.

2-2 THE REGIONAL CONTINGENCY PLAN (1510 PLAN)

As mentioned earlier, each of the 10 EPA regions and designated Coast Guard districts has a regional contingency plan, which is a regional amplification of the national plan. The Coast Guard is charged with developing the regional plan and providing the RRT chairperson and OSC in coastal waters. EPA is charged similarly in inland waters. Coastal waters are defined as those bounded inland by the terminal point of the "ebb and flow" of the tide. Seaward, the far edge of the *contiguous zone* [12-mile (19-km) limit] is the jurisdictional limit. By virtue of certain treaties and "Captain of the Port" authorities, however, the Coast Guard can extend its response to oil spills out to 50 miles (80 km), and in some cases 200 miles (322 km). The geographic

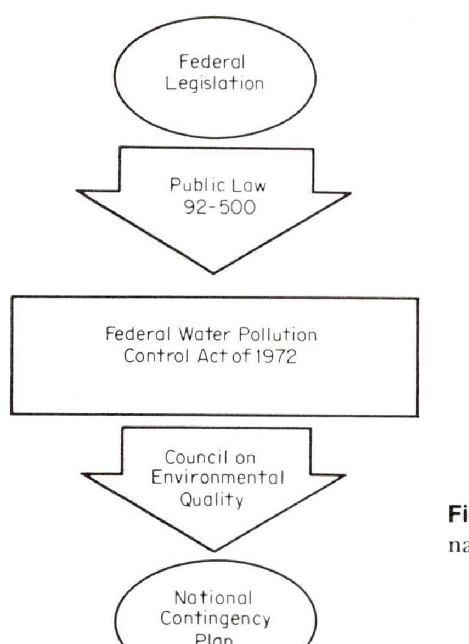

Fig. 2-1 Development of the national contingency plan.

division between Coast Guard and EPA authority have been in large part agreed upon by the agencies and are usually specifically described in the regional plans. Members of the RRT in any region are thus able to know prior to any spill event who will provide the team's presiding officer and the OSC.

The regional plan is a functional document which can be augmented by

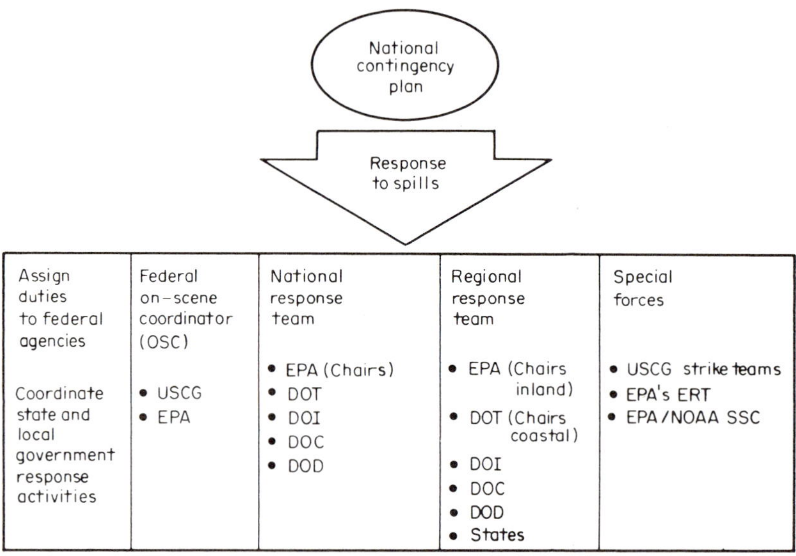

Fig. 2-2 Spill response organization under the national contingency plan.

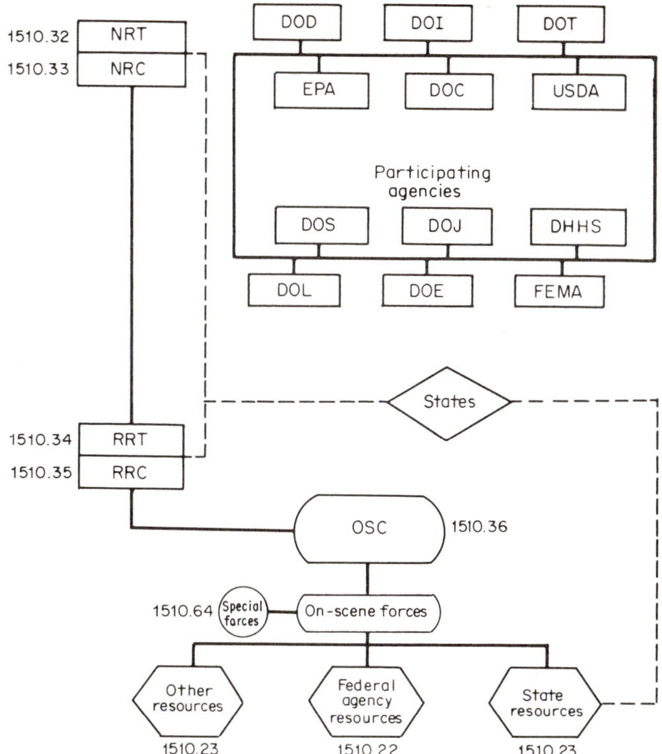

Fig. 2-3 Structure of national and regional response teams as called for in the national contingency plan.

state, local, industrial, and other plans in annex format. By submitting your plan to the appropriate Coast Guard district or EPA regional office, you can in fact make your level of government or other interest a functional element of the regional 1510 Plan.

The distinguishing feature of the regional contingency plan is the flexible membership of the RRT. Composition varies according to type of accident, location, interests involved, etc. Even more important, the state is a full primary member. The RRT is thus composed of representatives of the primary members of the NRT, representatives of the NRT participating agencies at the federal level, and representatives of state government (pollution authorities, civil defense, and state fire marshal). During one EPA Region IV annual 3-day practice session of the RRT, 51 state and federal officials from the eight Southeastern states met to drill on accident response. During any one year, this team, modified to deal with the type of accident involved, will convene on-scene to manage the cleanup of about 20 events in the Southeast. Similar activities on various scales take place throughout the nation. All spills of hazardous substances do not require RRT participation, but the plan, as well as the expert assistance, is always available as a guiding tool, to be used by even

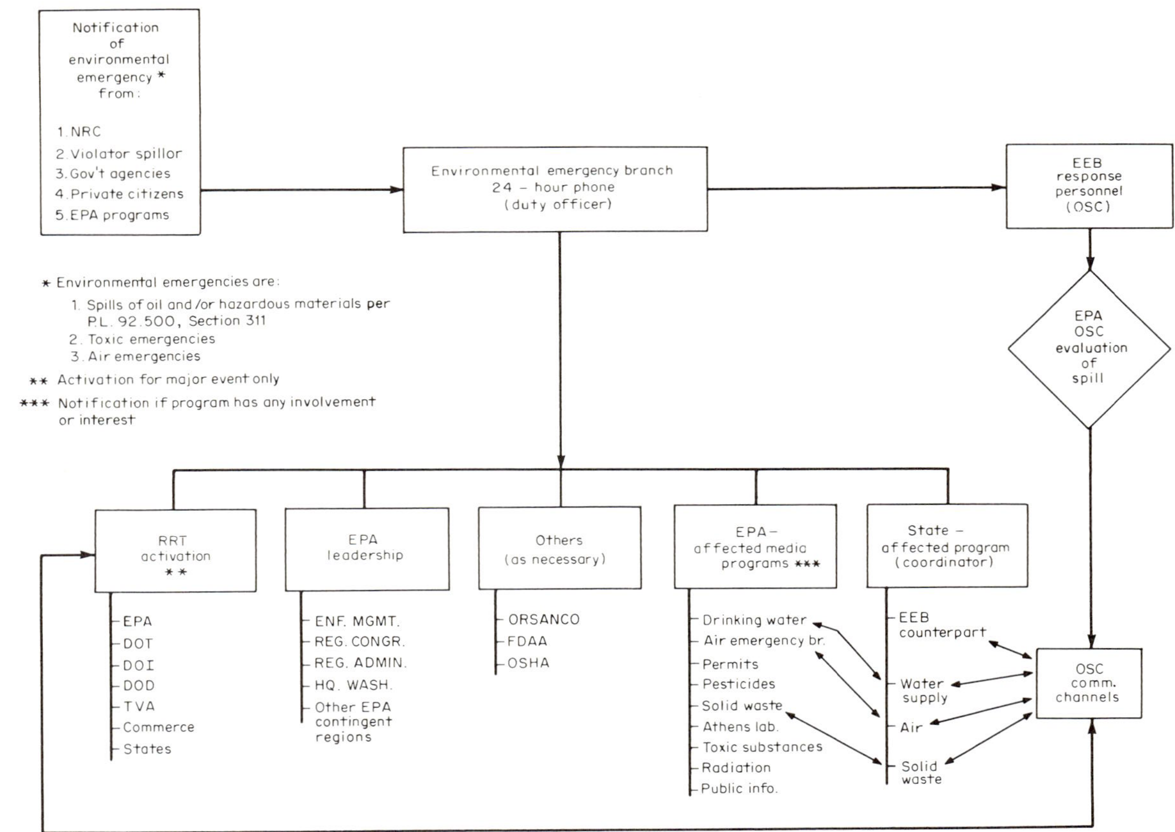

Fig. 2-4 EPA Region IV Emergency Communication System.

a single official responding to even the smallest event. The communication matrix for EPA Region IV is shown in Figure 2-4 to emphasize this point.

2-3 STATE CONTINGENCY PLANS

The Arthur D. Little study, backed by experience, reveals that the existence and adequacy of state oil and hazardous substances spill plans vary widely throughout the country. Some states have strong, well-documented programs; others have minimal ones or none at all. In the early 1970s, EPA published 40 CFR, Part 109, "A Guide for State Contingency Plans." The states' response to this in terms of spill contingency planning has been minimal. True, all states have disaster plans of some type, but they largely address the response to civil disorders, nuclear threats, and natural disasters (floods, hurricanes, and earthquakes). Such plans and the forces trained to manage them are vital, but to impose those plans on the cleanup of a chemical accident is simply not the answer.

During 1979 and 1980 a number of states struggled at the task-force and legislative level to deal with the problem. This state and local activity is natural and understandable. It could be harmful only if, in reacting to the modern siege of accidents, state legislatures began to formulate laws without cognizance of the federal laws that have existed and functioned for 12 years. The states must develop contingency plans *both* in cooperation with federal laws and contingency planning and in response to obvious needs. Poor state and local plans could tragically result in primacy arguments on-scene. For example, the federal government has been statutorily involved in the spill business for years. To tell a federal OSC that he or she has no authority on-scene, or to have this official detained at a roadblock, is to tell an FBI agent he or she is prohibited from being involved in interstate kidnapping. The other side of that coin is, of course, that the federal OSC cannot ignore the legitimate authorities of the state or local operation. The answer: plan together, work together. FEMA will be very active in this area during the 1980s and should provide a medium for planning. Along that line, why can't national, regional, state, and local oil and hazardous substances contingency plans all be workable parts of a master plan? There is more discussion of these relationships in Chapter 3, but for now we need to look at what a good state spill contingency plan should really consist of. At the minimum, a state contingency plan should have:

1 A statement of purpose and scope

2 Enabling laws

3 Identification of authorities involved

4 A mechanism for updating

5 An activity scenario (short but specific) for each element of state government involved

6 A merging doctrine, showing how the plan interfaces practically with federal and local plans

7 The predesignated state on-scene coordinator (SOSC) identified by name and/or position

8 Identification of a liaison official to work with the federal OSC and the SOSC

9 The state's 24-hour reporting number (maintaining this phone is absolutely critical)

10 A current list of key state and local phone numbers

11 Provision for local contingency plans by district, region, county, and/or key cities

12 Brevity (the federal plan should be no more than 50 to 75 pages long, excluding state plans and annexes. A good state plan should be 20 to 30 pages long, excluding annexes.)

13 A designated place where key officials can be found or at least where they check in upon arrival

Neither state and federal contingency plans should contain information that fills pages, changes overnight, or is generally available by looking in the local yellow pages. Long philosophical dialogues on methodology should also be avoided. A good plan identifies the appropriate people with the presumption that competent decisions will be made.

2-4 LOCAL CONTINGENCY PLANS

There are a few local contingency plans throughout the country that directly address hazardous substance spills, but not nearly enough. Authorities largely depend on the local civil defense organization, the sheriff's office, the public works department, the fire department, or some advisory group for emergency planning. But once again this planning is predominantly directed at events considered likely to affect that particular community, e.g., riots, fires, floods, tornadoes, earthquakes, or disruption of public services. The few communities that do have contingency plans specifically addressing hazardous substances accidents have usually been influenced by the presence of a substantial risk (a large chemical manufacturing complex) or a past event. But for the most part, plans found in the field today are not realistically applicable to chemical events. This is not to say that the emergency forces found locally are inappropriate; the function of the firefighter, the sheriff, and the civil defense official is an absolutely vital part of the cleanup and mitigation effort. It is the *application* of these functions that can be at times a problem.

Let us use the firefighter as an example. No group in this country is better trained and equipped to fight fires, but that is part of the problem. Training and planning mostly concern how to apply water to a fire, rearrange debris, isolate hot spots, remove and tend to injured, and protect personnel from smoke and fire. There are, however, a growing number of fires and potential explosions that need no application of water—where water, in fact, may well contribute to a major disaster. This involvement with chemicals is a whole new ball game. For example, a burning pesticide warehouse filled with 50 different compounds (chlorinated hydrocarbons and organophosphates) presents a real dilemma. The organophosphates can be oxidized and, while lethal in significant concentrations, can usually be managed even if washed into water supplies through storm drains and streams. Even contaminated soils can be treated to some degree. But chlorinated hydrocarbons are persistent and extremely costly to manage in the environment. If they are allowed to burn, the fire will yield noxious smoke, but short-term evacuation is necessary anyway. The warehouse may cost $200,000, but to protect the public from the pollution spread by water may well involve an expenditure of $1 million. Where the area can be secured, some gasoline fires may be less dangerous if cleaned up without the application of water. Very rarely should a burning tank car of vinyl chloride be extinguished, and of course some pressure containers cannot be quenched by water without risk of explosion. Water applied to the mixed chemicals usually found at a train wreck can at times be very dangerous; the cure for one ill may be the creation of a larger and more costly one in terms of risk to life as well as money. Local plans must embrace these concepts, and only training will guarantee them. Also, firefighting training must be more intensive for the volunteer groups. Previously, in the nation taken as a whole, these groups have not received the training and equipment they need and deserve.

The sheriff's deputy and the state trooper have challenging new roles at a roadblock during a chemical event; who should be allowed past the roadblock, what should the roadblock look like, and who will operate it? The real expert who will eventually resolve such critical priority issues may not be the man in the big car with endless credentials and a portable breathing apparatus; it may be the woman with a pocket calculator. Civil defense officials, local police departments, the sheriff's staff, and state troopers must also evaluate a whole new set of parameters for evacuation in the case of chemicals. During late 1978, 1979, and 1980, there have been increasing complaints from firefighters, police officers, emergency medical teams, etc., about lack of training. They know the problem well and are extremely concerned.

These issues cannot be resolved here. Each incident could and probably will someday be the topic of a book. (In fact, McGraw-Hill will soon publish a *Hazardous Materials Spills Handbook*. This book, written by 50 experts from all over the world, will be a tremendous aid to all.)

Again, the real key at the local level is contingency planning—contingency planning that will at least identify the new roles demanded of local officials by the increasing numbers of hazardous substances accidents.

In many states, legislation will be needed to formalize local contingency plans. Diffuse and at times overlapping jurisdictions must be covered by coordinated documents, not with intent to take away or disrupt longtime existing authorities, but rather to avoid duplication of effort.

Similar to the state plan, a local plan of 20 to 50 pages should be adequate. This plan should be distributed widely so that one will always be available on-scene. During a major event the three controlling documents—federal, state, and local contingency plans—should be available at the command posts. Each level of government should swap documents with the first greeting so that everyone knows where the other stands. Among other things, a good local plan should include:

1 A statement of purpose and scope.

2 Enabling acts and authority.

3 The identity and function of the officials involved (in the sheriff's office, fire department, civil defense organization, state police, EMTs, and social service organizations).

4 An evacuation plan with predesignated shelters and logistical support.

5 Identification of radio and TV stations that will continually inform the public during the initial trauma. These stations should be publicized periodically as a public service.

6 Identification of the predesignated local on-scene coordinator (LOSC) by name and/or position.

7 A mechanism for updating.

8 A document showing how the local plan interfaces with the federal and state plans.

9 Identification of a liaison official to work with the state and federal on-scene coordinators.

10 Continually updated phone numbers (home and business) of key officials.

11 A check-in location where key officials can be located or tracked once they have appeared on scene.

12 A method of identifying and accounting for *anyone* who may have authority to go beyond the roadblock. This can be preplanned by reviewing the state and federal plans, and can be coordinated during the spill response with the federal OSC and the SOSC.

2-5 INDUSTRY PLANS

Many industrial groups in the business of making, using, or transporting hazardous chemicals have developed contingency plans. Many of these plans have been forwarded to EPA regional and/or Coast Guard district offices. As a direct result of these plans, we see more and more competent response on the part of industry. Much of the cleanup technology is also developed here. We also see more and more willingness on the part of industry to do what is right in the case of an accident. There is a growing resentment on the part of industry, however, toward the inconsistencies of government at all levels.

Certainly industry cannot claim a totally clean bill of health, but let's pursue the issue for a moment. When the accident occurs, the responsible party automatically faces tremendous liabilities. Anything done subsequently on anyone's part can effect two things (among others) substantially: the direct cost of cleanup and the ultimate legal liabilities. With 40 different authorities (having 60 different priority concepts) giving the spillor perhaps 80 instructions—many of them conflicting—what is the spillor to do? If the spillor responds (and it usually does) to the agency with the largest club, is the public best served? How is industry to handle the politics of the situation? There have been cases where political figures appear to be actually running for office while on the accident scene. Is the public served well by this?

With exceptions, industry usually shows up immediately after the accident with trained cleanup personnel and a generally well-conceived plan of operation. It is also true that industrial priorities are based on such parameters as business continuity (getting the main rail line operational), costs, liabilities, and of course public, media, and political reactions. It is not uncommon for the spillor's plans to conflict with those of various governments, but it is becoming rare that a good, solvent company will actually defy authority to handle the situation its own way. There are times, however, when the spillor will say "No!" to a government official simply because another official with more—or apparently more—clout has ordered a different approach. Now, whose fault is that? Whose contingency program is breaking down—government's or industry's? More importantly, who suffers from all this?

As mentioned in Chapter 1, chemical expertise groups and specially trained response or strike teams are developing within the industrial sector. The chlorine industry seems to be a leader in this area, but the concept is spreading as specialists are being identified and trained in handling specific chemicals and their behavior in the field. We all must remember, however, that textbook chemistry is only one tool in the response to a chemical accident. The handy chemical cards or manuals, for example, that say "Stay away," "Evacuate the area," "Do not breathe," "Do not come in contact with," begin to lose value within a few hours after the accident because they don't tell how to clean up or complete the emergency situation. Cleanup and damage mitigation involve, in addition to chemistry, the fields of biology, ecology, toxicology, and pathology. How much can we breathe and for how long? How much can we come in contact with? How much can we leave in the soil? What are the problems concerning domestic or fishery water systems? Cleanup is a complex science, not simply a construction effort, and it is here that industry's contingency effort must be expanded. The public health and economic significance of the above is staggering, but we must start here, and we must do it now. It goes without saying that industry is in the best position to expedite this effort. Organizations such as the Chemical Manufacturers Association and the American Society for Testing and Materials, and research by EPA and others must tell those in the on-scene response business which values to use.

2-6 OTHER PLANS

Much has been said about the combined national and regional 1510 plan. It is now appropriate to discuss various other plans that have been developed to complement it. Almost all of the primary and many of the advisory members of the National Response Team have seen to it that oil and hazardous substances spill plans have been written for their agencies. Throughout the country officials have been identified through these plans to serve on the regional response teams. Many of these plans are annexes to the EPA and/or Coast Guard regional plans or are on file in either agency's regional or district offices.

Some independent agencies and commissions, lacking direct statutory spill authority but having significant vested interests in the spill business, have also developed plans. The Tennessee Valley Authority, the Ohio River Valley Sanitation Commission, and many others have very well thought-out plans.

In summary, this country has a contingency plan philosophy and has done much practical work in this area. There are admitted weaknesses; the system is not totally developed. But the mechanism is there, and the expertise and energy are there. These resources must not be wasted. The criticisms heard occasionally at the scene or later in hearings—that "Nothing was being done," "No one was in charge," or the cleanup effort was a "tragedy"—are largely unfounded. Such generalizations do not reflect the courageous efforts, particularly by local authorities, that have characterized most serious accidents in the past.

chapter
THREE

The Dynamics of the Regional Response Team in Action

3-1 A SPILL SITUATION

In Chapters 1 and 2 we discussed the RRT mostly in terms of its conceptual relationship to the contingency plan. Here we will be looking at how the team actually works during a spill, with federal, state, and local authorities participating fully.

To develop this discussion we will use an imaginary spill and problem outline. Consider a burning abandoned warehouse adjacent to a stream in a Midwestern state. This warehouse has been largely unknown to the local community. Here, without anyone's permission, an unidentified company (or individuals) has been storing unmarked drums of liquids and sludges retrieved (for a fee of $120 per drum) from a large industrial complex three states away. The first indication of fire came at 2:00 A.M. Sunday, October 12, when the local fire department was alerted by nearby residents to "bad-smelling smoke" coming from the unoccupied, unguarded facility. After the event was over and the case closed on December 12, the federal on-scene coordinator's log, in typical short-phrase but factual format, may have looked like this:

Oct. 12 *0200 hrs* Warehouse fire reported by residents ("bad-smelling smoke").

0210 hrs Local fire department is on scene. Explosion-like fire has erupted. Fire is white hot—fumes are overcoming initial respondents. Air-Paks are being used, but firemen are still becoming sick, especially those who tried to dam up aromatic liquid leaking from rear loading dock.

0230 hrs Central portion of building is burning out of control. Sheriff and local civil defense director arrive and request state troopers to help with initial evacuation of 1-mile radius (estimated 1000 people). During evacuation, officials find four bodies and 47 persons claiming illness from breathing smoke. Firemen have located one body in the outer perimeter of the fire (perhaps a vagrant or a bystander).

0250 hrs Adjacent buildings being cooled by water and believed secure. Fire water is leaving the scene by way of storm drains and is going toward Sundance Creek, the city's water supply. Civil defense director, fire chief, and sheriff huddle and decide to call the governor's department of emergency services (or State civil defense office).

0330 hrs The evacuation is progressing well except for several people worrying about medicine, dogs, and livestock, and two couples asserting their "Constitutional right" to be left alone. One state trooper was shot by a male resident who claimed he thought the trooper was a burglar. By 0430 hrs area should be clear of all but firefighters.

0400 hrs Fire in warehouse is still white hot. Reporters are on scene. Governor has been alerted and is en route. Chairperson of the county commission and two commissioners are on scene. Local civil defense director has been designated as LOSC* and has established a command post at the edge of the evacuation perimeter in a rented mobile home. Communications are being established via radio with the fire forces on scene and with the sheriff's deputies and state troopers operating the 10 roadblocks. Four EMTs are also on-scene and in communication with the two local hospitals.

0430 hrs The area is evacuated and is now secure. A roving patrol of state troopers equipped with self-contained air breathing apparatus is patrolling the evacuated area. The two local hospitals report they are at capacity with victims apparently suffering from both smoke inhalation and a blood disorder. Blood tests are being run and the poison control center 30 miles away at the county seat is sending a specialist.

0530 hrs Fire is still burning. White material washed from the building into an old sump at west side of facility appears to be burning while totally submerged in water. Five more firefighters hospitalized. Hospital reports three additional deaths with 10 patients advanced to the critical list. Governor is on-scene together with the local state senator, two members of Congress, and one local state representative.

0600 hrs EPA, Coast Guard, and state pollution control officials are alerted by the governor's representatives.

0605 hrs EPA activates the RRT and part of a communication system [similar to the one shown in Fig. 2-4]. Fire still burning. The county public works director has closed the city water system and ordered rationing. Fire reserves are dwindling. The hospital reports a total of 10 deaths at this time, but doctors now have a handle on the problem. Tests show cyanide poisoning, blood oxygen

* LOSC stands for local on-scene coordinator.

inhibition, and smoke inhalation. The hospital has only a few cyanide kits. By request of the RRT, the Air Force is flying in 100 additional kits from the state capital—ETA,* 0745 hrs.

0635 hrs The roving patrol arrested four persons suspected of looting and impounded one reporter who "got lost, missed the roadblock, just happened to wind up near the fire, and decided to take a few shots while that close." The reporter became sick at the police station, complaining of dizziness, nausea, and extreme weakness. A visual inspection by police officers revealed bluish lips, poor skin color, and pronounced perspiration. He was taken to the hospital immediately.

0720 hrs The fire has been extinguished. The LOSC has ordered all persons withdrawn from the scene and has called a meeting of all local officials. The decision is to await the arrival of chemical experts and the RRT [a wise decision at this point]. The local command post is now inundated with calls from media representatives located all over the country.

0845 hrs EPA arrives in the form of a federal OSC. With the OSC are the U.S. Coast Guard strike team and its command post, three state pollution control officials, and four more federal officials representing DOD, NOAA, Department of Interior, and FEMA.

0917 hrs The OSC immediately calls a meeting of the RRT† at the local command post. In attendance are:

1 The governor's representative.

2 Above-mentioned federal officials.

3 State officials. (The state water pollution representative has been designated SOSC.)

4 Sheriff.

5 Fire chief.

6 County commission chairperson.

7 Local civil defense director (LOSC).

Chairing this meeting is the federal OSC. Cochairing are the LOSC and SOSC. Media are excluded. At the 30-minute meeting it is decided that:

1 The next meeting of the RRT will be at 1200 hrs (noon). This will allow arrival of all experts.

2 The federal government (with state and local input) will manage the cleanup. Federal Public Law 92-500, Section 311(k) funds will be used.

3 A trained and experienced hazardous substances cleanup contractor will be ordered on scene immediately. (They were alerted at 0610 hrs by EPA and will fly two chemical experts in within the hour. Cleanup hardware to depart on call.)

4 LOSC will coordinate safety, evacuation, and social services.

5 The sheriff will coordinate security.

* ETA = estimated time of arrival

† See Figure 3-5, page 43.

6 The OSC will be given the timetable of events documented thus far and will assign the continuation of the log to the Coast Guard strike team, who will also manage the contractor.

7 NOAA will furnish weather data continually.

8 DOD will furnish logistical support for air monitoring and aerial surveillance, to include air transport of victims to remote hospitals.

9 EPA's ERT* which is en route will work with the SOSC to commence pollution and public health monitoring and overall cleanup of the badly contaminated area.

10 The OSC will assign the drinking-water problem to the state health official (public works director) and will request DOD to establish a temporary water supply. DOD will reassign this function to U.S. Corps of Engineers.†

11 A joint press conference will be held at 0915 hrs. Members speaking to the press will always be the OSC and/or the OSC press aide, the SOSC, and the LOSC or their press aides.

12 Investigation of the fire and the establishment of liabilities will be handled jointly by the DOJ representative (a deputy U.S. attorney or the FBI), and the state attorney general's office assisted by the sheriff's department.

13 State officials elect to work at both command posts, and communications are to be immediately established between the posts.

0947 hrs Adjournment.

0950 hrs Press conference.

1015 hrs The ERT, two chemical experts, and a medical doctor from Atlanta's Center for Disease Control (CDC) arrive. CBS, NBC, and ABC arrive together with 21 additional media representatives. There are now 221 people in the command post areas. But for some reason there are 300 vehicles parked in the vicinity, and mobility is becoming a problem. The sheriff agrees to handle this problem.

1030 hrs The OSC in conjunction with the Federal Aviation Administration (FAA) located in the control tower at county seat airport set up a restricted air cylinder, 1000 feet (305 m) in radius and 2000 feet (610 m) high.

1045 hrs A waiver is given by FAA for a special helicopter flight by a congressional delegation, the press, and the OSC. Area is still evacuated and no work forces are on scene. The flight is restricted to a 250-foot (76-m) radius and 500-foot (152-m) height. Local, state, and federal authorities continue to function in their jurisdictional areas, which are modified only when necessary to meet the more patterned needs of the RRT.

1200 hrs The hospital reported at 1115 hrs that deaths have been held to 12 and that the 65 other victims (total reported to date) appear to be stable, with improvement showing in many. All experts and contractors are now on scene. The RRT convenes. In attendance are the same people as before with the addition of the mayor's representative (we neglected to notify the mayor's office of the first meeting), the contractor, the FBI, state's attorney, the ERT, the doctor from

* ERT = emergency response team

† Corps of Engineers is often abbreviated as COE.

CDC, and two chemical experts. Again the press is excluded. Summary of RRT meeting:

1 The next meeting will be at 1400 hrs. Thereafter, twice daily at 0700 and 1400 hrs.

2 FBI and state's attorney are assigned two members of the ERT to go on-scene (with their special protective gear) and search for evidence prior to any cleanup. This will begin at 1300 hrs.

3 Press conference will be held at 1245 hrs (same representatives).

4 A complaint is issued by local officials that too many people are talking speculatively to the press. (One federal official not directly connected with the event has been giving poor information to the press.) The OSC is to contact the NRT in Washington and request that the official's central agency be contacted and that further press contacts be made through the RRT.

5 The helicopter overflight (furnished by the U.S. Air Force by request of the RRT) revealed that the area is still extremely dangerous. Two additional bodies were spotted in the center of the now collapsed structure. The ERT—because of the skin-penetrating chemicals involved and the special protective gear needed—agrees to get the bodies, but surveillance for cause of incident is delayed until 13 October. The overflight further revealed much smoke—a plume rising 100 feet (30 m) and extending northwesterly for 500 feet (152 m) before dissipating to nonvisible concentrations. Pools of liquid are all over the lot occupied by the structure. Discoloration of Sundance Creek was noted downstream past the water intake. Melted drums and viscous liquids are scattered about, and noxious odors were picked up in the helicopter. The press got their pictures. The major television networks are now insisting on an overflight. The OSC recommended it, and all agreed. All are in agreement that the area is too unstable for work to begin.

6 All agreed that the rest of the day should be spent refining our systems—communications, on-scene sanitation, Salvation Army support at the scene, and Red Cross at evacuation support centers. The spill area needs time to equilibrate.

7 The COE reported that a portable, potable water supply system (fire hoses, pumps, and rubber tanks) would be completed during the night. Water would be taken upstream of the spill, treated, and distributed from the makeshift clear well. The city's treatment plant is now contaminated. Treated water could be pumped directly into the city system at a point beyond the treatment plant. COE warned that they could furnish only one-fourth the city's normal demand and no firefighting capacity. The mayor said he would manage this by calling a public meeting at the fairgrounds the next day. He will broadcast spot announcements on TV and radio periodically until the water crisis is over. The State health department will check, certify, and monitor water quality.

1240 hrs Meeting adjourned.
1245 hrs Press conference.
1400 hrs Third RRT meeting:
Summary:

1 Four teenagers were caught inside the evacuated area. The sheriff issued a stern warning. Hospital reports total symptom remission among the sick. Autopsies on five, including the two removed by the ERT, indicate cyanide poisoning and blood oxygen inhibition as causes of death.

2 Helicopter flight scheduled for 0615 hrs, 13 October. The ERT, chemist, OSC, state pollution official, SOSC, and LOSC to participate.

1440 hrs Meeting adjourned.

1445 hrs Press conference.
Oct. 13 *0700 hrs* Fourth RRT meeting:
Summary:

1 Mass funeral set for 15 October.

2 Overflight reports some smoke but area seems much more stable. Coloration of Sundance Creek is better.

3 Air pollution monitors, encircling the area 500 feet (152 m) inside the roadblock on the northwesterly vector, report 2.6 mg/L of chlorine, 1.2 mg/L phosgene, and traces of ammonia. Water pollution monitoring reports indicate 14 mg/L of aminotoluene, 5 mg/L chlorine, 10 mg/L ammonia, 20 mg/L vinyl chloride and phenolic compounds. Traces of heavy metals were found in the bottom sediments, and there seems to be a total fish kill in Sundance Creek for 5 miles.

4 It has become clear that we have a long-term problem on our hands.

5 All agreed that the contractor, using only crawler equipment (bulldozers and front-end loaders), should move on-scene at 1300 hrs, move the debris around (avoiding chemical mixing as much as possible), and dike the entire area. We will then allow the area to lie idle another day, hopefully to re-equilibrate, thus avoiding any surprises when work forces reoccupy the area.

6 Two EMTs will move to within 1-minute response time of this four-man effort. Backing the EMTs would be two more teams, at 2-minute response time from the forward EMT location.

7 The FBI request permission to complete their investigation between 1000 and 1200 hrs; all agreed. The ERT will aid, as logged on 12 October.

8 The emergency water system is now functional.

9 LOSC reports that many support troops and decision-making officials need rest and sleep. The sheriff was asked to set up a rotating schedule for all locals; state and federal officials will do the same.

10 LOSC asked the sheriff to design and implement a color badge system for anyone going on-scene: Red for onsite anytime; yellow for work force; blue for accompanied officials or visitors. The sheriff will also maintain a log of all personnel going on-scene—time in and time out.

0745 hrs Meeting adjourned.
0750 hrs Press conference.
1400 hrs RRT meets briefly. OSC reports that initial work force has moved on scene and that there is no problem.

1410 hrs Press conference.

1800 hrs Work crew reports debris has been moved and area seems stable. A dike for surface-water retention has been erected around the entire lot. Since no runoff can enter the area, only precipitation will be contended with. NOAA reports months of freeboard are available for the contained site with respect to Sundance Creek.

Oct. 15 *0700 hrs* RRT meeting.

Summary:

1 LOSC has decided that the evacuation is no longer necessary. There is an objection from the health representative. The rest of the RRT is polled and decides in favor of maintaining evacuation. LOSC reminds all that people are hard to convince of the problem. He cites the stable appearance of the site, the lack of air pollution, and the lack of substantial evidence of imminent threat as factors making the people restless. Some are getting testy at roadblocks. The air pollution specialist testifies that both perimeter and on-scene air is showing only traces of pollution. Medical authorities say that experience is limited, but there is reason to believe that evacuation is harder on people than the apparent risks of reoccupation. The RRT is repolled and all concur with LOSC. Reoccupation is set for 1400 hrs.

2 The sheriff will maintain only four roadblocks. Civil defense will close down the perimeter area.

3 Operations have now evolved to cleanup. Public-safety considerations are yielding to considerations of public health and welfare and of pollution. Air pollution efforts are no longer emergency-oriented. Water pollution monitoring will continue to be top priority, with soil monitoring and disposal considerations becoming a principal concern.

4 At 0800 hrs a technical evaluation team with appropriate breathing equipment and skin-protection gear will move on-scene and determine if the debris can be separated into two categories. If so, the team will identify and color-tag the debris. Material that can be safely deposited in local landfills will be tagged blue. This material will require some testing, but most likely will prove to be the remaining building materials and empty dumps. The other debris soaked by water and chemicals will be hauled to the nearest hazardous materials landfill and the trucks will be detoxified. [See Figure 3-1.]

5 At 0800 hrs the contractor will begin detoxification of the water-treatment plant. The treated water will be discharged to the sanitary sewer system if a treatability study permits. Filter sand and sediment sludges will be taken to the local landfill if chemical concentrations are below 1.0 mg/kg. Steam-cleaning water will be discharged into the sewage-treatment system. Zocco Labs, Inc., will do all monitoring of the chemical levels during these two operations. EPA's Solid Waste Program will design a plan for contaminated soil and liquid disposal using soil-chemical data from Zocco. This study should be completed by 28 October. [See Figure 3-2.]

0755 hrs Press conference.

Oct. 18 *0800 hrs* RRT meeting. [NOTE: RRT is now made up of the local public works director, Department of Interior, NOAA, EPA, Coast Guard, and

Fig. 3-1 Debris and debris removal after hazardous chemical fire.

state pollution and public health officials.] EPA now has six on-scene representatives and the state four, representing among them the following programs:

EPA	State
1 Environmental Emergencies (OSC)	1 Health Department
2 Solid Waste	2 Solid Waste
3 Air Pollution	3 Water Pollution
4 Pesticides	4 Enforcement
5 Drinking Water	
6 Enforcement	

The size of the RRT has stayed about the same, but the expertise configuration has changed substantially.

Fig. 3-2 Oxidation of organophosphates.

Fig. 3-3 Landfill being prepared to receive hazardous substances.

Summary of RRT meeting:

1 The debris has been removed and the surface liquids have been sampled and compartmentalized for treatment. The debris proved to be a problem when the out-of-state hazardous substances landfill operation required that tests be run on each truckload of debris. [See Figure 3-3.]

2 The sand has been removed from the water-treatment filtration system and disposed of in the hazardous materials landfill. The water trapped in the plant was tested and found to have low concentrations of the chemicals (listed earlier) that had been released into the city sanitary sewage-treatment plant. Steam cleaning of the plant is now under way. Superchlorination (20 mg/L) will be employed to flush valves and piping. The resulting water will also be released slowly into the sewerage system.

3 Comprehensive testing and treatability studies will begin at 0800 hrs, 19 October on the soil mass and the various impounded liquids on-scene. Samples will be pulled from both site and stream and flown to EPA's lab for analysis. [See Figure 3-4.]

0925 hrs Meeting adjourned.
0930 hrs Press conference.
Oct. 27 *0800 hrs* RRT reconvenes.
Summary of meeting:

1 The water-treatment plant returns to service at 0900 hrs, 27 October. This part of the problem has ended.

2 There has been trouble in sending samples by air. A sample broke en route and leaked on adjacent baggage. The bag's owner filed a complaint with the airline, and subsequent investigation revealed that an official had checked "undeclared" liquids in glass containers aboard a commercial airliner. The airline paid damages, but the FAA has issued a notice of intent to file criminal charges (under

Fig. 3-4 Water samples must be taken by those proficient in that specialty.

49 CFR) against the official. The RRT has asked FAA to advise it of all regulations involving shipment of hazardous materials.

3 FAA will immediately issue to RRT an abstract on emergency shipment of chemicals, oxygen tanks, environmental samples, and other restricted or regulated items.

4 Tests have been run on samples shipped to EPA's lab, and results are as follows:

- **(a)** Within the five liquid reservoirs there are four distinct mixtures, requiring different treatment techniques.
  - (1) One pool or reservoir will require drumming and shipping to an approved incinerator (with EPA-approved air bag). This mixture is principally chlorinated hydrocarbons and vinyl chloride.
  - (2) One pool is principally rain and wash water and may be drained into the sanitary sewer system.
  - (3) The third pool is principally organophosphates and will be oxidized by superchlorination.
  - (4) The fourth pool involves elemental phosphorus. This will be taken to the army base and detonated by Army EOD on a remote artillery range.

    Only traces of aminotoluene, chlorine, phenol, ammonia were found in the pools.
- **(b)** Soil is highly contaminated with all of the above chemicals in varying amounts to a depth of 1.0 ft (0.31 m). Aeration by tilling is out of the question; the chlorinated hydrocarbons are persistent, possibly up to 5 years, and there is direct leaching as evidenced by stream monitoring. Thus 1000 cu yd (765 m^3) will be taken to the "secure" out-of-state hazardous wastes landfill.
- **(c)** The stream is protected by a trench intercepting the leaching material and a dike diverting runoff. Daily sampling (to be continued for 2 months after site restoration) is now showing no chemical in a concentration greater than 0.05 mg/L. The state will also monitor water-treatment plant

stream for 1 year. This is the rationale for reopening the plant for domestic usage.

5 Adjourned.

1000 hrs Press conference.

Nov. 5 *0800 hrs* RRT meeting [See Figure 3-5.].

1 Summary: Site cleanup going smoothly, but publicity has caused adverse feelings in the state receiving the waste. Officials in that state were notified, but local media have insinuated that "back door dealings" had made their community the receptor of "another state's mess." Local talk show has agreed to allow OSC to present the case history to the community at 1930 hrs, 8 November. Rumor is that an injunction will be sought to prevent further disposal in that state.

2 Meeting adjourned.

1000 hrs Press conference.

Nov. 8 No RRT meeting.

2200 hrs OSC reports to command post that TV appearance went well. There is good reason to believe the job can be completed.

Nov. 21 *0945 hrs* RRT meeting. All present: local, state, and federal.

1 Site is clean; stream is clear.

2 State will continue monitoring.

3 RRT resolves that the emergency is over.

Dec. 2 OSC presents OSC report and log to NRT for review and comment.

Dec. 3 OSC presents log and independent investigative reports to EPA legal staff for enforcement and federal funds recovery. Total cost: $928,600.00.

Dec. 4 OSC attends governor's debriefing (at state capital) coordinated by civil defense. Attending are members of local, state, and federal governments, most of whom were RRT members.

Dec. 12 OSC attends Senate overview hearing in Washington.

CASE CLOSED

Fig. 3-5 A regional response team in session.

3-2 COMMENTARY

While the spill event described above was fictitious, it was made up of aspects of events that have actually occurred. The log leaves the reader with the impression that an accident had occurred and tragedy had accompanied it, but that a smooth, organized response, despite a number of small setbacks, minimized the effects. The real story, however, is that these accidents do happen with increasing frequency and the response is *less* coordinated and effective than suggested by the example. Although there are management and regulatory tools available at all levels of government to deal with such events, too often the response is ad hoc, uncoordinated, and characterized by a duplication of effort as well as competition for credit in the press. The ultimate loser, of course, is the local public. Nevertheless, let us consider the result in comparison with the alternatives.

The event now over, we are left with an area that is environmentally clean, although not a public health paradise. The site is quarantined for a year, and perimeter-monitoring wells and stream monitoring will reflect any encroachment of residual pollutants on areas beyond the site. EPA will more than likely list the site as a "Hazardous Waste Dump Site . . . being monitored," a condition which will keep the site in the public eye for several years. Once the quarantine has been lifted by the state pollution control authority, there is every reason to believe that the site will be safe for most uses. Was it worth a million dollars? Of course, if we consider the protection afforded the public, and the various illnesses that could have arisen from the site for years. Remember, pollution and public health effects are no longer viewed only in terms of how acute or lethal they are, but also how chronic; i.e., how long we will suffer or potentially suffer from the event.

Now review this exercise from your own perspective and reread the log, putting yourself in an overall coordinating role. Don't argue with the technical details, the language of the log, cleanup chemistry, etc.; the numbers, measures, methods, and even the safety parameters are subject to variation on a case-by-case basis. What is paramount here is to use what is available effectively.

Before taking the exercise apart piece by piece, let's review personnel who may have been involved on-scene. Here is a partial listing of groups that are involved with increasing intensity in hazardous substances events.

EPA

- Solid Waste Program (RCRA)
- Environmental Emergency Program (Section 311)
- Drinking Water Supply Program
- Toxic Material Program (TSCA)
- Public Affairs
- Surveillance and Analysis Program
- Legal Staff

DOT (USCG)

- Marine Environmental Protection
- The Strike Team
- The Public Information Assistance Team
- Marine Safety Office (MSO)

DOD

(Could be one or more of several agencies: COE, DOA, Navy, Army EOD Team)

DOC (NOAA)

- Weather Bureau
- Scientific Support Group

DOI

- Fish and Wildlife Service
- Conservation and Recreation Service
- U.S. Geological Survey
- National Park Service

USDA (Forestry)

HHS (CDC)

DOJ (U.S. Attorney)

Federal Railroad Administration

National Transportation Safety Board (possibly FBI)

Bureau of Explosives

Federal Emergency Management Agency

State Agencies

- Water Improvement Commission (Air and Water)
- Health Department (Solid Waste and Water Supplies)
- Civil Defense
- State Patrol
- National Guard
- Governor may appoint a special representative

Local

- Mayor
- County Judge (in certain states)
- Civil Defense
- Police
- Sheriff
- Press (local and national)

Political

- Varies, but always involves members of national and state legislatures

Affected Parties

- Company official (if located)
- Shippers and/or product owners
- Industrial expertise groups: CHEMTREC, etc.
- Property owners and local public
- The injured
- The Audubon Society, Save the River, and other environmental groups

The entire exercise recorded in the log reflects a management-oriented operation using the existing tools of expertise and regulatory authority. Just one official, even one with some extraordinary authority, acting unilaterally and outside the patterned exercise, can literally ruin the entire exercise. He or she can interrupt priorities, put the public in undue jeopardy or fear, and actually cause physical harm.

Events during the hours from 0200 to about 0530, on 12 October, which we will call phase 1, typify the initial response to most kinds of accidents. In this accident, however, hazardous substances were involved. In retrospect we can say it would have been far better to have had little or no water added to the fire; costs could have been cut by perhaps 80 percent. But until we are ready to pay those extra taxes and buy our fire forces more sophisticated equipment and training, we must not be critical of this aspect of spill-emergency response. Only about 10 percent of all fires involve hazardous substances, and in perhaps 50 percent of these fires, water must be used to limit the scope of the fire. Proper response to the remaining chemical fires (only a small percentage) will require tremendous amounts of training, in terms of the first 3½ to 4 hours of the event.

Phase 2 of this exercise, beginning at about 0600 hours on 12 October and continuing for 6 days, warrants serious scrutiny. As you recall, in Chapter 1 we discussed the laws and operational concepts of various government functions, and in Chapter 2, the contingency planning available. These all went into effect with the phone call to EPA at 0600 hours. It is noteworthy to mention that the owner or operator of a facility must, *as soon as* he or she has knowledge of a spill, call the U.S. Coast Guard's hot line and report the accident. The federal criminal sanctions incurred upon failure to do this are a $10,000 fine and a year in jail, or both. (There are perhaps 20 pages of legal definitions of the terms *discharge, permitted facility, waters of the United States, imminent and substantial threat,* etc., which we will not discuss in this book. Obviously, however, the laws and regulations are just not that well defined at this writing.) The point to remember is: There is a federal reporting requirement, and in the future the federal family will more frequently be notified as soon as the local agencies are.

In any case, after the first few hours of panic and response, the emergency safety period, or phase 1, is over. Phase 2 is the establishment of the RRT and development of the cleanup methodology. This phase in the exercise ends on or about 18 October. After that date, the exercise basically becomes the implementation of the RRT's instructions and winding the operation down, that is, it goes into phase 3. Those familiar with the national contingency plan must not confuse these three phases of the hazardous substances incident with the five phases of contingency operations outlined in the plan. The latter five phases are contingency groupings and assume compatibility of all levels of government. The three phases referred to in this book refer to the timing of governmental activities, functions, and jurisdictions. This is a key distinction.

In phase 2 of the exercise it is the critical interface of authorities that merits discussion. Even the most loyal and dedicated local officials are overwhelmed by the sheer numbers of people that begin arriving at 0845 hours (refer to the log). They are tired mentally and physically, and usually are not adequately equipped. But they respond because they must. This is where they live, and the people involved are their constituents, friends, or kin. At times an official from another area of government presents an attitude that is simply not acceptable. It then becomes difficult for any federal and/or state official to move in and assume a leadership role without at least appearing to the weary local official to be exhibiting this same attitude.

On the other side of this issue are the federal and/or state officials functioning under a specific statutory authority. They are confused by what appears to be resentment by the local authority. For example, in Chapter 2 (page 23) we quoted the national plan: "The OSC . . . should exercise great caution in allowing civilian or government personnel into the affected area. . . ." This is federal law and is subject to congressional question if not executed by the OSC. How does the sheriff (the chief law enforcement authority in the county, assuming home rule government) react to this? Another example can also be found in Chapter 2, Section 2-1, under Public Information Network: the RRT has a clear, legally mandated duty to maintain a full free-flowing press function. In most states, however, the civil defense organization speaks (by executive authority) to the press. There is no need to discuss the implications to the public of poor, incorrect, or conflicting press releases. How can we resolve these issues? There is only one logical forum: the RRT.

The presiding officer of the RRT, through the RRT's OSC, has the federal authority to formally delegate local functions to local authorities. The LOSC, for example, should be appointed at the first RRT meeting.* He or she can then redelegate functions to the obvious local groups or officials. The question arises: Local officials have authority anyway; why assign something that is already a duty by law? The answer to this question is the key to the management concept of this book. The contingency plan program of total patterned

* The term *OSC* (federal) is established by law and won't be changing soon. The terms *LOSC* (local on-scene coordinator) and *SOSC* (state on-scene coordinator) are the author's invention. You may well wish to develop another title, such as *state coordinator, local team leader,* or *protem boss,* etc. The title *commander,* however, is not recommended because of its specific usage in military context.

response embraces the idea that all actions are in unison—a symphony, so to speak. The civil defense official with evacuation authority now has the support of the RRT. Without this endorsement by the RRT, there is unilateral decision making, and that can be extremely risky. Evacuation can be the subject of argument and confusion, and, more recently, of law suits. Most civil defense or sheriff's personnel, forced to evacuate a group of people out of necessity, welcome a technical review and endorsement or recommendation by the RRT. The local officials have not surrendered any authority, but have merely joined the team. This writer has yet to see the local residents or press criticize the local official who is exercising authority and performing duties as part of a team action. With the same team concept in mind, why can't there be a three- or four-person press team speaking for all levels of government and other interests at regularly scheduled press meetings? And why can't they be quartered together answering phone calls and/or questions directed to their area of involvement.

Referring again to the exercise, at the first RRT meeting at 0845 hours, shouldn't the RRT have reviewed the actions up to that time as a first order of business? Was the civil defense representative satisfied with the size of the area evacuated? Was the sheriff happy with the perimeter security? Not mentioned often in the log, however, are the several occasions on which the RRT members were polled by the presiding officer for their impressions of specific procedures and how they were conducted. This polling is not a vote but simply a means of assessing the views of the experts.

As a final note in this review, consider the value of being able to report to the governor's debriefing and the U.S. Senate overview hearing that yes, there were some minor problems. There were also errors, but they were committed within the scope of the RRT. All were at fault, but no one was negligent. Everyone was informed, and *look at the final results.*

chapter FOUR

Laws and Contingency Planning: Some Suggestions

Even though at this writing, and without Superfund legislation, the current federal response to accidents is limited to spills or discharges into "waters of the United States," the nucleus for a proper response does exist. This is true despite the lack and uneven quality of state and local plans at this writing. The concept of planning for accidents is very much alive in this country.

Government interests are aroused; the public has seen to that. Agencies that have had congressional mandates and statutory authority for some time are now making efforts to execute their responsibilities. Agencies that have little or no authority but that clearly do have interests—and even some agencies having very remote interests—are getting actively involved. Calls are being made daily to EPA and the Coast Guard regional offices by all of these agencies, which are asking to be made at least advisory members of the RRT. This surge of interest, that actually began about 1977, is extremely positive. But with the interest comes the need for the regulated integration of these activities into the overall management scheme.

As an example, a top-level federal official in Washington, making a call to a regional office and asking "What are we doing at Crestview?", is *in effect* asking the official of that region to get involved, even though he or she has no direct authority or responsibility in this event. This usually develops into several phone calls or a site visit. Multiply this by 100 (if you include relatively new state and local groups), and you can begin to appreciate the problem. Consider the politician, also aroused by an event or series of events that seems particularly important, holding hearings and proposing new legislation and/or authority in the area of accident response, sometimes while the spill response is actually in operation!

It is obvious that the OSC and RRT cannot manage these activities. It would be absurd, however, to argue that all outside interests should be ignored. Even those who conceived the original national contingency plan had vision enough to make it flexible and promulgate the philosophy that one day the current plan would be a viable integral part of a master plan. Obviously, under current federal, state, and local laws, the authorities and jurisdictions empowered to perform at the different emergencies are diffuse and, at times, overlapping. But at present, those seeking an organized preaccident means of becoming involved and exchanging information are frequently hard pressed to find plans that allow them to do so; thus the growing confusion is understandable.

The answer to this problem is mind-boggling and far beyond this writer's ability and vision. Generally speaking, however, contingency planning will eliminate the confusion that currently exists both among those who are involved and those who seek to be. The following comments may help point up specific areas of need and may encourage those who do have the vision, ability, and position to act.

1 The National Oil and Hazardous Substances Pollution Contingency Plan is excellent and has served well where its use was appropriate. It needs expanding to embrace *all* emergencies involving oil and/or hazardous substances. (Remember the Waverly, Tennessee, incident mentioned in Chapter 1, Section 1-3?) This will take legislation, but there is no reason to believe that the President's Council on Environmental Quality could not, in conjunction with the NRT and appropriate federal agencies, modify the plan. As mentioned earlier, FEMA in conjunction with EPA has funded an investigation of certain aspects of this modification. This study was completed in 1980.

2 In addition to current legislation efforts, there should be some form of federal legislation requiring the states to have contingency plans which are compatible with the regional and national plans. The study mentioned above is also concerned to some degree with this need. Of course, there will have to be a method of funding to allow the states to develop the plans.

3 In this same vein, there should be federal legislation requiring the states to develop adequate plans at least down to the county level. In large cities (Standard Metropolitan Statistical Areas) there should be plans supplementing the county plan. Once again, funding is required.

4 Those making, selling, using, or transporting hazardous materials should be fined for the accident (based on liability). The fine should be placed directly in the contingency fund for cleanup and/or should become funds for state and local plan development. There is a direct incentive here to prevent the accident and to provide for cleanup. An arrangement for quantifying liability is not impractical, and it is reasonable to believe that a fair schedule of fines could be developed, based on the accident's potential effects on human health. The suggestion here is that the fine serve as payment for the accident, rather than as a punitive measure. Of course the cost is ultimately passed on to the public. But experience has indicated their willingness to pay for environmental and public health protection if it is a question of *accidents,* not negligence, and if it can be achieved by a well-articulated and efficient system. Industry has often shown that it does not object to the fine concept per se; nor does it object to the cost of cleanup. What industry strongly objects to are arbitrary fines and excessively expensive cleanups when it is obvious that part of the expense is chargeable to poorly coordinated governmental activities on scene.

5 Each federal agency with legal authority in the hazardous substance business must be identified and, perhaps by presidential order, be required to briefly outline this authority in a formal statement. This statement should be annexed to the national 1510 plan. Each agency with this responsibility must further have a set of internal ground rules in which those authorized to act are identified and their response activities are described.

The first four of these suggestions are concepts on which at least some action was taken in 1979 and 1980. For example, the Superfund bill has statements that relate to item 4. The FEMA-EPA Study involves the concepts mentioned in item 3, and the 1980 edition of the national contingency plan calls for the activities mentioned in items 2 and 3. But follow-up—or lack of it—could make or break each one. However, in 1971, for example, EPA published a regulation pursuant to P. L. (Public Law) 92-500 calling for state contingency plans and outlining minimum criteria for such plans. As of this writing, only a few states have developed serious pollution emergency response plans of any kind. Only time will tell how serious we are as a nation about giving prior planning attention to these accidents.

Were the five possibilities discussed to become realities, fine tuning would still be necessary to achieve ultimate efficiency. Consider the possibility that in the future *expertise units* or *response spheres* could be developed within each government agency. Each response sphere would respond to and work with accidents in a particular category. There could be a rail accident sphere, highway accident sphere, fixed facility sphere, an existing hazardous site sphere, and a special task group for the accident that doesn't fit any category. Once the type of accident is established, response would be limited to those previously identified by each agency and level of government as responsible for that sphere. Of course we are years from such a possibility, and our immediate reaction to such a proposal must surely be to ask how much it will cost. We are talking about several billion dollars in governmental costs. But can anyone really doubt that small, well-trained governmental units comprising federal, state, and local personnel, each trained in the special situation being confronted, would be efficient? We read daily about the prognosis for cleaning up many of the messes we have ignored for years: $10 million to begin working on the Love Canal site, and perhaps $400 million per year to clean up the several thousand additional sites we could locate right now. How much money will be spent in government alone over the next few years in organizing an effort to handle this single sphere? Aren't we really discussing *efficiency* throughout the first three chapters of the book? For the past few years, when faced with a problem, we have responded to *that* particular problem. Then when we have been faced with another problem of a different (but equal) concern, we have responded to *that* problem. The result is a collection of laws that is mind-boggling. It is time we review the whole emergency system from top to bottom.

There are five categories of disasters that can occur:

1 War
2 Natural (hurricanes, floods, etc.)
3 Nuclear (energy-related)
4 Political and economic (national sabotage, riots, nuclear attacks on the country, power blackouts, and financial crisis)
5 Hazardous substances emergencies:
 (a) Spills (land, water, air)
 (b) Hazardous waste disasters (such as Love Canal)
 (c) Plant accidents (hazardous or toxic substances)

We have at least a handle on categories 1 through 4. There is a governmental management scheme for each of these. FEMA, for example, has recently absorbed the agencies that prepare for, regulate, and manage categories 2, 3, and 4. War is obviously well covered. It is category 5 that is so dynamic, occurs so frequently, and is subjected to public scrutiny daily. How long has it been since you purchased a daily newspaper and did not read about one of the events mentioned in category 5? Yet it is here that we are somewhat diffuse in terms of management regulations. As we have noted, there are current efforts at both the federal and state levels in many of the areas outlined above. Now is the time to pull together and bring these ideas and concepts to consummation.

chapter

FIVE

Prevention

In concluding Part 1, this chapter discusses the merits of a regulatory system for the prevention of accidents. Until optimum efficiency is achieved in the area of prevention, we cannot expect maximum efficiency in the areas of accident response and cleanup. There is clear evidence that a strongly enforced prevention program does reduce accidents. However, in order to examine this issue, we will first look at various categories of emergencies.

5-1 THE FIXED FACILITY

A variety of accident potentials exist at the fixed facility (manufacturer, user, or handler). Here are some of them:

1 Equipment failure
2 Inadequate design
3 Inadequate maintenance and inspection
4 Inadequate physical security; sabotage
5 Inadequate facility housekeeping
6 Human error: poor training, negligence
7 Acts of God

Types of accidents include:

1 Classical spills
2 Effluent discharges

3 Fires and explosions
4 Gaseous releases
5 Soil contamination
6 Waste disposal techniques

Safety, of course, should be built into virtually every activity that has a spill potential, and, with safety, some degree of accident prevention. This involves actual construction features as well as operator training and management commitment. Take, for example, the federal regulation 40 CFR, Part 112: Oil Pollution Prevention. If a non-transportation related facility has more than 1320 gallons (5.0 m^3) of oil storage above ground (provided no single container has a capacity greater than 620 gallons (2.5 m^3)) or more than 42,000 gallons (159 m^3) oil storage capacity underground, and that facility can be reasonably expected to discharge to waters of the United States, it must have a Spill Prevention Control and Countermeasure (SPCC) Plan.

This plan must be designed by a registered Professional Engineer and must document positive prevention features such as secondary containment structures, rearranged topography, management commitments, operator training, safety, and security. The Engineer must certificate his or her plan, thus announcing its competency and professionalism as a matter of state law. The plan should address most if not all of the seven accident potentials associated with oil listed above. The companion regulation, for hazardous substances should be in effect in the early 1980s. It offers both government and industry regulated techniques in handling many chemicals at facilities.

The Clean Air Act, the Toxic Substances Control Act (TSCA), and the Resource Conservation and Recovery Act (RCRA), all involve some form of management of hazardous chemicals. TSCA and RCRA are most comprehensive in this area. State pollution and emergency laws are very broad and embrace prevention as part of the accident response and enforcement procedure. Local fire, police, zoning, and building regulations view prevention as a viable part of safety programs. Certain Occupational Safety and Health Administration (OSHA) procedures concerning safety are in reality prevention techniques. In EPA regions where there has been significant enforcement of the Oil Pollution Prevention Regulation, there has been a substantial reduction in oil spills in both numbers and volume. The finalization of hazardous substance spill prevention regulations, if they eventually apply to fixed facilities, promises the same positive results.

5-2 THE TRANSPORTATION INDUSTRY

A very large percentage (perhaps as high as 80 percent) of all spills of hazardous substances is transportation-related. Railroad, trucking, vessel, and pipeline companies appear to be the most vulnerable to various types of accidents. The same seven factors that affect fixed facilities apply to transportation facilities, but the probability of occurrence skyrockets when the factor of mobility is added.

Trucking

The growth of the trucking industry in the past 15 years has been unbelievable. With the development of the interstate highway system serving as a predominant economic base, we have all witnessed this phenomenon. Truck-stop cities have sprung up across the countryside, with motel complexes, restaurants, huge fuel stations, shopping centers, ground traffic control towers, and radio systems. Naturally, the chemical- and oil-hauling portion of the industry has kept pace. Accidents involving trucks carrying liquids and gases have become so frequent that response crews have been unable to keep up with cleanup. There have been some frighteningly close calls involving the wrecking of trucks loaded with hazardous substances near densely populated areas. But so far this country has been lucky—very lucky. Because truck accidents usually involve less than 10,000 gallons (37.9 m^3) of a single chemical, response is more regulated, and damage mitigation and cleanup are more predictable. On the other hand, the public uses the same roads, so the potential danger for people is always acute. A second vehicle is involved in perhaps 50 percent of all hazardous substances truck accidents, and securing the impact area as well as traffic control can be far more complex than that required in rail or vessel accidents.

In terms of prevention, the trucking industry is regulated at the terminal or transfer station by 33 CFR, Parts 154 and 155, Spill Prevention regulations. The Coast Guard administers this portion of Public Law 92-500. En route the vehicle is regulated as to loading, capacity, handling, and labeling of hazardous materials. These materials are categorized by the Department of Transportation as to how flammable, explosive, corrosive, or poisonous they are. In recent years, the term *hazardous materials* has come to include both the toxics and a new category—*hazardous substances.* These newer pollutants, while regulated at fixed facilities and terminals, are yet to be regulated by prevention laws while in the moving vehicle. DOT has agonized over how to accomplish this, and no one can argue the complexity of the task. Some day soon we may see strict operator regulation, mandatory training, competence testing, and periodic license evaluations, all concerning the hauling of hazardous substances. In the meantime, one thing is certain. The company and/or driver that loads up with a chemical, no matter what it is, better drive with caution; the liabilities are tremendous.

Vessels

Inland tows are not immune from carrying hazardous cargoes. The same accident-potential factors apply to inland tows carrying hazardous cargoes as they do to trucking. But the added factor of public waterways as the traffic medium brings emphasis to the public health aspects of the accident. The tug that is involved in an accident while pushing a tow of chemicals—chlorine, toxics, caustics, acids, etc.—presents a massive problem. We are talking about huge ports, dense populations, domestic water supplies, and, of course, commercial fisheries. The potential spill is in millions of gallons (thousands of cubic meters), and the effects are hard to predict or even to calculate after the accident occurs. As with trucking, spill prevention regulation for vessels is generally limited to terminal facilities. Again, the design of a positive, overall prevention program is a tremendous task and will require a massive effort involving a broad spectrum of expertise. In all fairness it must be stated, however, that while the accident potential is huge in terms of size of spill and public involvement, statistics show that the number of vessel accidents is very small.

Railroads

The biggest dilemma in the transportation industry concerns the nation's railroads. We read almost daily about a tragic railroad event, and the public seems more apprehensive about this kind of accident than any other. Yet with a few exceptions, the railroads as an industry are very responsive to their accidents, and many in this industry argue that they don't deserve the criticism they frequently receive. The president of one of the large railroads once told the author that railroading per ton-mile of cargo handled is the least polluting industry in the United States. Some may take issue with this, but the industry is sensitive to the public, and there is evidence that they are trying to address the problems. The Louisville and Nashville Railroad (L&N) has spent millions cleaning up its railroad yards in Atlanta and other cities; so have other railroads. Tracks are being repaired all over the country. Research and design are underway into methods of developing penetration-proof—double-skinned or heavier—cars. Yet the rail accidents continue to occur, and the public is enraged. What is the problem then? Is it track foundation, light-weight rails, excessive speed, too many cars on one train, poor hardware, lack of operator training and education, inadequate track surveillance? As with vessels and trucks, the prevention regulations (except at fixed facilities) are not yet available.

Pipelines

Although cross-country pipelines are not used in the transportation of chemicals, oil and fuel are still occasionally spilled from them in large quantities. The need for regulatory attention is generally the same here as it is in the transportation industries discussed above.

We will further discuss these transportation modes in Chapter 6. There is no doubt, however, that prevention is the key, and no matter how tough the chore, much of our attention and energy must be poured into developing methods of accident prevention.

5-3 WASTE MANAGEMENT

Involving both fixed and transportation-related facilities is the considerable problem of *waste management.* The chemical industry generates millions of gallons of wastes daily—residual solids, sludges, liquids, and mixtures of these. For years burial has been the principal disposal technique. In May of 1979, EPA announced that the scope of this problem was staggering. It has been estimated that there are 20,000 hazardous burial sites endangering public health and that the cost of mitigating them will run as high as $50 billion. Love Canal and the Valley of the Drums are sites we hear of on *60 Minutes.* The problem is not exaggerated; it is real and must be confronted. Across the country there are abandoned warehouses filled with drums of chemical wastes, open pits of oil and polychlorinated biphenyls, buried drums, and covered pits filled with liquid. If we were able to run a trace on all the chemicals made, used, and on hand for the past 10 years, there would be a staggering quantity missing. "Moonlight disposal" is not new, but as we tighten regulations it could possibly grow into an enormous problem.

Let's look at what's really happening. Industry is aware of the problem. Landfills that are approved to handle hazardous wastes are scarce and very expensive when available. Even material cleaned up from spills is difficult to dispose of properly. I don't want a hazardous materials landfill next to my house, do you? But there will be a growing number throughout the country, and they will be near someone's house. The difference is that this new generation of landfills will be carefully designed, vigorously monitored, and always in the public's mind. And in spite of all objections, these landfills will be absolutely necessary. If proper disposal facilities are not available, we had better guard our roads at night. We have been subjected to the illegal dump for too long. Those in the regulatory business are aware of this, but the activity is much larger in scope than might be assumed. There are even unpublished claims that organized crime is involved. Consider this example: A large, well-intentioned company accumulates 50 drums of a highly toxic chemical waste. Observing the various laws, it calls in a solvent, well-advertised waste reclaimer (who is licensed to do this work and has an approved incinerator and a small, approved landfill) and contracts for disposal at $200 per drum. This reclaimer then discovers by testing procedures that it can't burn or bury the waste. It calls another company that says it can. For $150 per drum, this perhaps less solvent company purchases and transports the waste to its always-reliable landfill for disposal at the usual $75 per drum. But the landfill is now regulated and cannot take this material. A few phone calls later, the reclaimer finds that only one disposal site in the state *can* take it, but only for $210 per drum. Not to be defeated, this company calls the local new, small but eager oil reclaimer in the area. Without full knowledge of the facts, the oil reclaimer makes a deal for $100 a drum. After discovering a week (and some hundred phone calls) later that it has purchased a real hazard, it dumps the waste in the nearest stream. This of course is unacceptable. But who is ultimately at fault, morally as well as legally? Before we blame the oil reclaimer or even the barely solvent chemical reclaimer, aren't they part of a system that has existed for years? Caught between the need for hazardous waste disposal and the absence of ample authorized disposal sites, they now find themselves in an impossible position. And the day we put all of the small reclaimers out of business, watch out. There won't be a mosquito in any stream in the area—or a fish. What solutions are on the horizon?

The Resource Conservation and Recovery Act, a waste management scheme that will trace and account for hazardous wastes from the cradle to the grave, with industry ultimately responsible, is one of this country's most exciting new laws. Its basic set of implementing regulations was promulgated in May 1980, and EPA began enforcement immediately. Prevention is ingrained in every aspect of these regulations. There will be much paperwork and widespread frustration, but as a nation we can do no less. In the near future you will also be hearing of a government-industry effort to construct a huge waste incinerator on an oil platform off the coast. Think of the possibilities this undertaking offers. If we can eventually have a number of these incinerators, and if they are clean, well managed, and safe for air and water, think of the reduction in land disposal acreage. There will be no need for a Valley of the Drums, Love Canal, or such an incident as described above. Fire departments, sheriffs, National Guard, civil defense workers, and pollution and industrial officials will all know where and how to get rid of deadly chemicals and polluting toxicants. Equally important, everyone will know the price to be paid. As we identify and police a realistic method of disposal and enforce prevention, don't we all benefit over time in terms of economy, public health, and safety?

part
TWO

Technology

chapter
SIX

The Accident: Forms, Effects, and Contributing Factors

6-1 BASIC FORMS OF EVENTS

Accidents that prompt governmental response take many forms in terms of the products spilled, the method of spill (or potential spill), where spilled, and the subsequent effects on humans and the environment. As suggested in Figures 6-1 through 6-10, it is important to have thought about the many possible forms of accidents before evaluating your own role and attempting to develop a technical response to an actual accident. Note that the word *accident* continues to be used for general purposes. Clearly the abandoned drums filled with chemicals (Figure 6-1) represent more than an accident. And the drums in Figure 6-2 were actually secured in the trees (during a flood) by pollution officials to prevent them from floating away to unknown locations. Subsidence of the river, however, left an interesting recovery problem.

In Figures 6-1 through 6-10, notice the factors of terrain, weather, air movement, and the proximity of the event to towns, houses, or streams. Consider the perhaps lethal gas clouds, the closeness of the river, and the precarious position of the cars in the derailments; the intense heat, oncoming traffic, and homes involved in the truck accidents. The sinking barge and floating boom constructed in the attempt to contain diesel fuel on the river suggest the difficulties encountered when dealing with streams and rivers. The chemical or oil influence on the surface of a swamp stream raises the

Fig. 6-1 The Valley of the Drums, Shepherdsville, Kentucky, 1979.

question: How far and wide will it burn? The drums in the trees are rare as a form of accident, but the discovery of a warehouse full of abandoned drums or a field covered with chemical-filled drums, is not. Consider this:

- There are perhaps 20,000 (some EPA estimates range as high as 50,000) unmonitored hazardous waste sites in the United States.
- Several thousand hazardous chemical spills that are discovered by the federal government each year when in fact there is no enforceable federal law requiring reporting. In truth, there are perhaps 15,000 chemical spills of varying significance each year.
- There are thousands of in-plant accidents every year involving chemicals that are toxic to some degree.

Fig. 6-2 Chemical drums in trees after 1978 flood of the Ohio River.

Fig. 6-3 Chemical-coated stream on fire.

When the word *significant* is used to define a spill, it should be viewed as an incident that has some measurable impact on the human environment. Again, look at Figures 6-1 through 6-10. Only two lives were lost in these incidents, but each was *significant* in terms of this discussion.

6-2 THE EFFECTS OF CHEMICAL ACCIDENTS

The basic effects of any spill are its measurable impacts in the areas of health, environment, sociology, economy, and politics. The ultimate tragedy is death. Figure 6-11 shows the removal of a victim killed by a chlorine gas cloud. The

Fig. 6-4 Oil successfully boomed on a slow-moving river.

Fig. 6-5 Wrecked truck loaded with an explosive chemical.

victim was 450 yards (412 m) from the source of the cloud, a cautionary reminder for those who have a tendency to get too close. In terms of people killed, we have been extremely lucky in the United States. But there have been a number of frightening near-misses. The truck of bromine shown in Figure 6-5 killed only the driver and her passenger. If the accident had occurred a few miles further north on the same highway, it would have been directly adjacent to a number of occupied dormitories at a major university. An exploding truck of liquid propane gas on a causeway near a large metropolitan complex in Florida could have occurred one mile (1.6 km) further north and, instead of killing just the driver, could have killed the hundreds of people crowded into low-rent housing units. There are dozens of similar stories.

Consider the public trauma caused by the 1979 Three Mile Island nuclear reactor event. Evacuation was similar to that of a sizable chemical event, and

Fig. 6-6 Storm drainage after a chemical truck accident can be a problem.

Fig. 6-7 Terrain is an important consideration.

no one was killed. Yet thousands were in the streets chanting, "No to nukes!" Alarm, overreaction, and speculation were involved, but the public was justifiably worried about the potential long-term contamination and unknown health effects. Death is a concern, yes, but also the long-term biological and unknown health effects must be evaluated.

It is unrealistic to assume that because a chemical is insoluble, viscous, or dense it will not penetrate the ground and perhaps lie there for years as a substantial danger. At Kingston, Tennessee, in 1973, an accident involving the spillage of 1200 gallons (4.5 m^3) of polychlorinated biphenyl and trichlorobenzene resulted in a $1,700,000 cleanup. One water well was contaminated as far as 100 yards (91 m) up-gradient. Concentrations of PCB in

Fig. 6-8 The effect of surface winds.

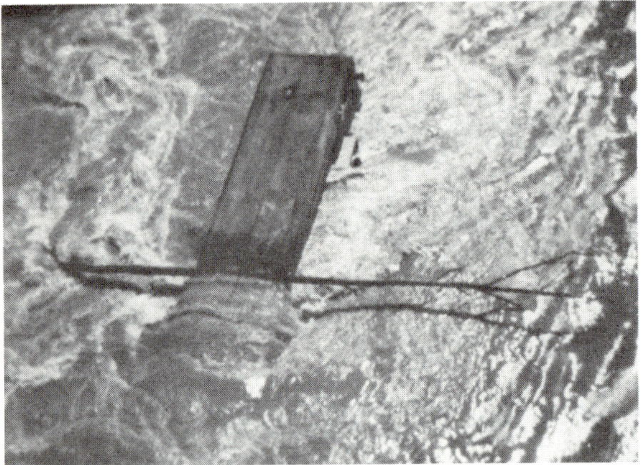

Fig. 6-9 The significance of river current.

the soil were measured up to 2960 mg/kg at depths of 18 feet (5.5 m). Of course the debate rages back and forth concerning the effects of PCBs on humans. If you are interested in these arguments, read very carefully the book *PCB Poisoning and Pollution,* edited by Kentarb Higuchi and published by Kodansha, Ltd., Tokyo.

Beyond human effects lie the massive biological and toxicological impacts of spilled chemicals. Figure 6-12 depicts the familiar result of many spills. But what about damages to the life-support systems of the fish? How long does it take a lake or a stream to recover from a traumatic shock? Because there is a growing quantity of literature on these subjects, they are not discussed here. There is little doubt, however, that *cleanup* is a technical concept that must include containment and recovery of chemicals. There is more discussion on this subject in Chapters 7 and 8, where we review your roles and cleanup technology.

Fig. 6-10 The consequences of poorly stored chemicals.

Fig. 6-11 The ultimate tragedy.

6-3 FACTORS THAT AFFECT ACCIDENT SCOPE

Often the accident site is not geographically limited to the immediate work area or the area evacuated. One town's instant salvation may be the next town's dilemma. The movement of danger out of the immediate area is of continual concern. Many factors are involved with this problem—some that can be controlled and others that cannot.

Weather

Weather of course is a critical factor in the response phases of any spill. Obviously it cannot be controlled, but it can be considered during priority discussions. Weather science is now so sophisticated in the United States that reliable reports such as precipitation forecasts, local temperatures, and surface-wind and high-altitude-wind data are made continually available on

Fig. 6-12 Other kinds of victims.

scene through the National Oceanographic and Atmospheric Administration. It is not impractical to obtain such information every 5 to 10 minutes during critical operations, and the data are amazingly accurate in even remote locations. The federal OSC will always have access to this service through the NOAA representative on the RRT.

In gaseous events, winds are critical. Surface gusts can be such that the work site may have to be abandoned in an instant. Steady, directional winds that have brought about the need for evacuation may, on the other hand, be a blessing at the work site. It is always a good idea to have six or eight wind streamers placed at low and high points in the immediate work area. An observer should always be assigned to monitor these during operations in which workers are vulnerable to shifting concentrations of on-scene gases.

Rain has been called a mixed blessing. Regardless of the blessing, it is always a concern. The rain that may dilute a chemical, cool potential reactants, and reduce the dispersion of a gas cloud can also serve as a vehicle to mix reactants, transport chemicals to streams, aid soil penetration, and generally cause sloppy, dangerous working conditions. Again, while rain is an uncontrollable factor, it can be planned for, and with quick reactions and the simplest of tools, its effects can be dealt with.

Excessively high temperatures increase the potential for chemical reactions, aid volatilization, and are a critical fatigue and stress factor for workers on scene. The best-trained individual may react to heat stress by shedding vital equipment. As the fatigued worker cannot be expected to recognize his or her own peril, this must be monitored visually at all times. No one really knows when or why a person's courage and dedication will exceed judgment and common sense. Rapidly changing temperatures are also extremely dangerous where perforated tanks of volatile gases are involved. A work scene may be subjected to "burps" and sudden releases of lethal gases anytime the surrounding temperatures rise sharply. The suddenness of such an event is shocking and can surprise the most experienced worker.

Terrain

How many natural sites have you seen that do not eventually drain into some body of water? The apparent absence of a channel, swale, or conduit means only that we haven't searched well enough. Unless the area is a swamp or lake, it has drainage of some kind. Even areas that allow temporary storage (such as small fishponds) eventually drain. As a consequence, essentially *every* transportation-related (and most non-transportation-related) hazardous substances accident is a *potential* spill into waters of the United States. If the material will not run directly to a stream of its own, it will do so when aided by rain or fire-control water. As with most natural factors that affect an accident, terrain can be both a hindrance and an aid. Areas with critical relief components such as cliffs or steep inclines are not only difficult to work in but offer little help in surface-liquid containment. Yet this situation may well resist or minimize gusting surface winds.

Soils

Soil characteristics are important in predicting penetration, absorption, and of course working capabilities. Extremely fissured or rocky soils together with sandy or dry very plastic clays provide good conditions for the immediate penetration and transportation of nonviscous liquids into water systems. But highly organic soils, heavy leaf mold, or peatmoss soils are tremendously absorbent and may well aid spill mitigation by sorbing and buffering certain chemicals. It should never be assumed that soil bodies are homogeneous, especially if any priorities are to be based on that assumption.

Fire

Conventional fire training is not always adequate in chemical situations. Fires spawned from chemical reactions, temperature changes, and the application of water itself make the chemical accident extremely difficult to handle. Fire may also at times be a blessing in disguise. Fire is visible, and if it can be determined that the particular fire is isolated and is consuming all matter exposed to it, then a continuing, controlled burn may be practical. But there is no room for surprises—such as hidden containers or pressure tanks—in this approach. In fact, chemicals such as vinyl chloride may, because of self-ignition or polymerization characteristics, be safer when allowed to burn, despite the emission of toxic fumes. What is really being evaluated in such decisions is predictability and risks, weighed against such factors as the spreading of a difficult-to-treat pollutant and potential long-term soil contamination. Explosions of course are a number one concern. Always unpredictable, the possibility of such an event weighs on everyone's mind from start to finish. People who have been involved with fires for years, however, contend that few explosions in field situations are instant. Firefighters seem to develop a ninth sense in anticipating them, and I have seen firefighters bail out and run on gut instinct alone just seconds before an explosion. Some say there is something in the characteristics of the smoke—an intensified motion—that warns. The point is, 90 percent of all explosions give some warning, even if brief. The remaining flash-type explosions are usually characteristic of a situation which should not have been closely attended in the first place. The risk in this 10 percent (such as at Waverly, Tennessee) is too great to warrant development of skills in this area. *Don't get too close!*

Debris

All serious accidents are accompanied by varying quantities of debris. Wood, metal, plastics, and contaminated soil are all part of the problem. Contending with this material, which at some point must be moved and properly disposed of, can impose additional factors of concern. The movement of large pieces of metal, for example, could, without proper care, cause the puncture of an otherwise dormant pressure tank. Torch cutting must be done carefully and only after the local chemical atmosphere has stabilized. Heavy equipment must not be allowed to "track" the area, creating ditches in which chemicals can mix, unless that is part of the properly designed cleanup technique.

People

The most variable factor of all is the well-meaning, curious observer. He or she seems to be in the way of every swing of the boom, so to speak. To have to stop a 'dozer or crane from moving a chemical tank because someone is standing in the way is absolutely inexcusable. Officials who literally bulldoze their way on scene are not just offensive; they are an extremely dangerous obstacle to the work force. This is a serious matter to be carefully considered by all.

Time

No factor will be more significant in the response to a hazardous substances accident than the passage of time. How time is spent in the early phases of the event will ultimately make or break the overall efficiency of the total response. In the very early moments, actions are characterized by speed. Controlling the advancing fire, removing the injured, and evacuating the area are quick, instinctive reactions that will always accompany the accident. Once these things are done, the obvious move is to retreat to the limit of the evacuation area and wait—wait for perhaps 6 to 8 hours after the last significant explosion or subsidence of the last major fire. Without fail, chemicals involved in various kinds of accidents will mix, explode, burn, yield toxic gases, and even kill, but at some point in time the entire event will normalize, i.e., equilibrate, to some degree. While we have waited for this state of equilibration that will allow us back on scene, liquids have fully mixed, soil penetration has become significant, and whatever runoff was possible has occurred. In short, pollution and health hazards have advanced. The question is, however, could we really have done much of any real significance in these 6 to 8 hours except expose people to a high risk of death or injury? Cleanup technology is advancing to the point that now this 6 to 8 hours is not nearly so critical. The safety afforded by waiting far outweighs any gains that could have been made by continuing a precarious operation.

chapter
SEVEN

Cleanup Forces and Your Role

7-1 WHAT IS CLEANUP?

Because the term *cleanup* is used throughout this book, we must now explore it in depth and clearly understand its meaning. In the context of this book and with respect to the overall management concepts outlined herein, *cleanup* will be taken to mean *the reestablishment of a damaged area to reasonable usefulness.* As we move toward that goal, all of the following are involved:

1 Safety:
  (a) Classical
  (b) Emergency
2 Protection of public health and welfare:
  (a) Water supplies
  (b) Soil contamination (acute)
  (c) Air emissions (acute)
3 Continuity of community livelihood
4 Environmental protection (pollution)
  (a) Stream pollution (ecological aspects)
  (b) Soil pollution (residual long-term aspects)
  (c) Air pollution (chronic consideration)
5 Confident reuse of the damaged area

It is obvious then that *cleanup* is not merely quenching the fire, removing the injured, burying the debris, or removing the wrecked equipment; it is all of these plus *how to do it* that is on the public's mind today.

The EPA and state pollution authorities are getting more involved in post-spill biological assessments and long-term monitoring of some of these sites. Kingston, Tennessee, the site of a 1973 spill of PCB, is studied every 3 years to determine:

1 Biodegradation
2 Spreading of the material
3 Effects of natural weathering
4 How safe the site is

To the author's knowledge, this is the only long-term study *of its kind* in the United States at this writing. At Whitehouse, Florida; Trion, Georgia; and a number of other locations where persistent chemicals have been spilled, the state and local pollution and health officials, in conjunction with EPA, continue to analyze samples from monitoring wells constructed in a circular pattern around the sites. At Youngstown, Florida and Dothan, Alabama, as well as many other sites where dangerous but less persistent chemicals were spilled, the damaged area has been quarantined for periods of time (usually not exceeding one year). Each site where significant quantities of hazardous substances are spilled must not only be purged of as much of the material as economically reasonable but must also be monitored. If we fail to do this, we allow such sites to become potential Love Canals on a smaller scale.

In the early 1970s this country became aware of the magnitude of the oil spill problem. The shocking realization hit all of us; not only were we losing hundreds of millions of gallons of product each year, we were doing significant damage to the environment. Surprisingly, we discovered that while the more visible and dramatic offshore spills received worldwide attention, the smaller, more frequent, inland spills were quietly causing equally significant harm. Statistics published periodically by EPA and the Coast Guard indicate that more than 50 percent of the oil spilled in the United States is spilled in inland streams. These are *reported* quantities; one can only guess what the true totals would be. The Congress decided in 1970 that the policy of the United States is that no oil or hazardous substance shall be spilled into its waters. This policy, together with the amendments to the Federal Water Pollution Control Act, has resulted in the government activity seen at an oil spill today.

Reflecting back over the past 10 years, one can readily see how far we've come as a nation (and around the world for that matter) in oil spill cleanup. No longer do we depend on a coffee can nailed to the end of a willow stick to dip oil out of a stream. Nor do we use skimmers that tip over and sink. Hay and straw are no longer our principal sorbent and containment materials. While in 1970 there was only a handful of competent, full-time cleanup contractors to handle oil spills, today there are hundreds. Oil cleanup is a developing science, and efficiency improves yearly. In Enoree, South Carolina, during May 1979, over 300,000 gallons (1,135,500 L) of oil were recovered of the 500,000 gallons (1,892,500 L) actually spilled into the Enoree

River. This river was flowing at a reasonable rate, even at the wide and deep sections. Such recovery percentages are becoming routine for the inland spills. Ocean spills, however, remain very difficult to clean up for obvious reasons.

What then is the "state of the art" of hazardous substances cleanup? Why do our response capability, technology, and enforcement efforts lag at least 10 years behind those involving oil, when the words *oil* and *hazardous substances* are always mentioned together in our federal pollution spill laws and regulations. The answer, perhaps, lie in the size of the task. Reviewing our definition of the term *cleanup,* it becomes obvious that to develop appropriate regulations is extremely difficult. At this writing, there is a tremendous effort on the part of EPA's top management to resolve this problem of what to, when to, and how to clean up. What materials, for example, are *harmful?* Which ones must undergo rigid cleanup and "secure" disposal? As an example of the difficulties involved, how do you develop a list of hazardous substances that is comprehensive enough to embrace the entire problem and at the same time avoid discriminating against particular chemicals that are less harmful than others, or harmful in some situations and not in others? There are solvents (such as benzene) that are so noxious that simply smelling them will render you considerable harm, but when spilled, these same chemicals are so volatile that little residual is left after a short period of time. Yet the same chemical may be a known carcinogen. What parameters should we use to determine the chemical's harmfulness: people, plant life, microorganisms, fish? Cleanup technology will advance slowly until these key issues are resolved, or at least better understood.

Suppose by some stroke of luck we were to resolve much of this problem and could begin to formulate a realistic program for practical, economical, and consistent cleanup. One of the first murky pictures that would clear up is *your role.* The firefighter would know in advance which chemical fire to extinguish. Members of civil defense, the National Guard, the sheriff's department, and others would have a better handle on evacuation and safety. Industry would know to what extent cleanup should be carried, and pollution and health officials would know how to recognize *harm* in the field. Cleanup hardware and techniques would develop overnight. And of equal importance would be the immediate advantage we would have in the area of proper disposal.

We are not there; make no mistake about it. But in the early 1980s, look for signs indicating that hazardous substances spill cleanup has begun catching up with the capabilities we now have in oil spills.

7-2 WHAT IS YOUR ROLE?

If you can accept the author's concept of cleanup, you can begin to envision how you can best apply your authority, responsibility, and expertise to the accident scenario. In Chapter 3 we discussed the three phases of a hazardous substances accident. Let's look at them once again in terms of your role, and at the same time keep in mind the fictitious accident we used as an example.

Phase 1

This is the initial stage of response, generally covering the first 4 to 6 hours after impact or discovery of the fire or explosion.

Federal and state agencies

The EPA, the Coast Guard, and FEMA should be the first agencies notified at this level of government. In *inland* situations, the EPA is charged under the law with furnishing the OSC. For the significant spill, the EPA OSC will usually make between 9 and 20 phone calls of notification. Many of these calls are internal and are purely routine. As soon as possible the OSC will notify the regional response team (RRT) and, in the case of EPA, direct the members to assemble on scene. (The Coast Guard, who would chair the team in coastal waters, feels that the RRT should operate at a remote location. There is an argument for and against each method so we won't dwell on the subject further.) The various agencies should spend these hours getting their technical data together and responding. Each primary agency on the RRT, including the state civil defense and pollution authorities, should be keenly aware of its roles as clearly outlined in the 1510 plan.

Local agencies

For the first few hours the response is a local one, and all activities during this period are critical to the type and amount of effort required for the entire exercise. Basically the hazardous substances accident involves a new and perhaps unknown twist to your normal function at a nonchemical accident. The people are the same, the human emotion and panic are similar, but the chemical or chemicals involved make it different.

Civil Defense Coordination is your most obvious role. Your training in communications and your knowledge of the local people and on-site terrain make you extremely valuable. In most states, civil defense personnel do not have police-type authority, but are vested instead with the responsibility for warning and alerting the community. You should participate (if not take command) in the initial evacuation. Set up the command post in a visible location upwind of the spill (if you can determine prevailing surface winds) and at the edge of the evacuation zone. Meet with the sheriff, highway patrol, and fire team leader as soon as possible. Taking no more than 5 minutes, you must set up the coordinated procedures of initial response. If you are the local on-scene coordinator (LOSC), then be available to coordinate. Employ your local contingency plan which by now you—the county commission, sheriff, fire chief, Red Cross, Salvation Army, highway patrol, National Guard, and/or Army Reserve—should have formalized in writing. If your state or county and/or city laws have established another official as LOSC, then be at his or her service. Don't assume roles, and be extremely careful in carrying out your own. Whatever you do, get the planning done now. Decide who is going to be the coordinator; don't wait for the accident. As part of preplanning, make sure your gear is ready—that the light plant, radios, trucks, jeeps, etc., are all ready. A second role is training. Some local official must train local people in responding to such accidents. Civil defense training for nuclear attack and tornado response is becoming well known at the grass roots level all over this country. Shouldn't we train equally for accidental spills of hazardous substances? Isn't the statistical probability of such events as great and greater? Remember, this training must embrace fires, explosions, some basic chemical information (manuals, etc.), and most important, the actual awareness of each person's role. If we drill in preparation for tornadoes, why not for accidents involving chemicals?

The Firefighting Agency and Fire Marshal The fire department is usually, among the first, if not the first, on scene. Is the typical fire department really ready for this kind of event? Fire department managers all over the country are preparing themselves for this new era. Fire marshals are asking EPA officials to take part in their training programs. At the 1978 International Hazardous Materials Conference in Miami, Florida, a surprising number of fire and EMT personnel were in attendance; the same was true for the 1980 conference held in Louisville, Kentucky. The message is clear; everyone is anxious to become more proficient. Fire departments are keeping records of technical assistance that is available and the phone numbers of key spill officials. If you aren't doing this, please do it now. Post those CHEMTREC, EPA, and Coast Guard 24-hour numbers where the night watch can see them. Obtain from Chapter 10 the type of information you may need, and order it today.

Once you realize you are confronting a chemical fire, you must—in cooperation with civil defense, sheriff, and spillor—find out what the product is. Get the manifest, call the company, or with all due caution look at the labels or markings on the tanks or containers. Once you know what the product is, call CHEMTREC, EPA, or the Coast Guard. Give them your information and receive immediate aid. You may wish to compile your own data base, but keep it simple and practice using it. If there are unidentifiable chemicals involved, evacuation and perimeter cooling of noninvolved facilities may be the best policy. There is no real, hard and fast single answer to such a problem, but defensive actions are the best in such a case. It is always dangerous to get close enough to a railroad chemical fire to put water on it. The quantity and complexity of mixed chemicals are such that explosions can propel steel fragments for distances recorded at 2500 feet (762 m). Always coordinate with civil defense, the sheriff, and highway patrol. Know where everyone and everything is; be a part of your local contingency plan. As you practice fire response, add some practice for the chemical incident. Find out who the LOSC is and work with him or her.

Sheriff and Local and State Police (Highway Patrol, State Troopers) Your role will always be safety-oriented, but your police authority is absolutely essential. Some states may want the sheriff to be the LOSC because of home-rule government concepts. Under such rule, the sheriff is by law the chief law enforcement officer in the county. Participation in the evacuation is vital because of your training in handling people. It can be a tough job, and there are always some legal ramifications, but contrary to common beliefs about constitutional rights, once the official decision to evacuate has been made, people *can* be evacuated. During one huge oil terminal fire in DeKalb County, Georgia, in the early 1970s, people who chose to physically resist evacuation and those who reentered the area were fined heavily by the courts. A word of caution would be to avoid negligence or what could later be charged as negligence, but do not shrink from duty in anticipation of the charges an irate citizen may make later. The most tiring and burdensome responsibility will be manning the roadblocks and keeping people out of the area, but these things must be done. Evacuation is brutal on people, and those who are sick or on special medicines must be given consideration as the accident stabilizes.

If you are not the LOSC, seek out him or her and coordinate your activities. Be sure you have the contingency plan and conduct periodic training sessions. Generally (but not always) the state police and local city or county police work under the coordinating direction of the sheriff. If your local plan is different, fine, but be sure it is understood.

County Commissioner, Mayor, or County Judge During the early hours, your most obvious task is to monitor the conduct of the forces implementing the local contingency plan. You certainly have responsibilities and authorities, but very few of you are trained in this area. So take the broader view; look for duplication of effort, conflicts, etc. Be the "Balm of Gilead" during these critical first few hours. Get together with your LOSC, be continually briefed, and visit the evacuation shelters. This is reassuring to the people hardest hit by the event. Help the local officials prepare for phase 2 of the event. A huge contingent of state and federal officials is only moments away. Meet with the federal on-scene coordinator (OSC) and the state on-scene coordinator (SOSC) when they arrive. Help them locate their command posts and arrange a meeting with the local officials as soon as possible. This will help the OSC in calling the initial regional response team (RRT) meeting. These people are coming to assist *your* community. That is their *only function;* help them out.

Spillor The spillor, if known, has a primary duty of making known to the LOSC or *any* local official exactly what chemicals *may* be involved. Failure to do this within a few hours is inexcusable. We hope that in the future there will be stiff federal criminal penalties for such a failure. Your role, of course, then becomes one of financing cleanup. During phase 1 you will always be primarily responsible to the local officials, but it is paramount that only *one* person be giving you instructions until the arrival of the federal OSC.

Red Cross and Salvation Army Have your initial response coordinated with civil defense and the LOSC. Red Cross, if you are to handle the shelters, you must preplan the occupation and service of the shelters. Salvation Army, if your call to service is to aid the troops doing the cleanup, then be prepared. A valuable function of your groups would be to help coordinate local clergy who are disseminating news of death and injury to the next of kin. This is a high-priority item, and at times the local forces that normally do this for a routine accident are now too busy on-scene. If at all possible, you should not allow this kind of news to reach the media prior to notification of kin.

Emergency Medical Teams or Service No role is more critical. In most jurisdictions your role for the specific event is coordinated through the local civil defense. If this is not the case, then find the LOSC and work directly through him or her. Be sure you are visible, and make it clear for whom you are working.

Phase 2

Phase 2 begins perhaps 4 to 6 hours after impact and lasts from 2 to 6 days. There is always a distinct beginning to this phase. After 4 to 6 hours of firefighting and evacuation, the scene usually begins to stabilize. The scope of the fires is known, the extent of damage is becoming apparent, explosions are more predictable because of perimeter cooling, and at best there is a lull when most forces can be withdrawn to the local command post area. By now it is known that there are chemicals involved, and, in the best case, what they are. Help should now be arriving from the state and federal sectors.

Phase 2 is characterized by a merging of federal, state, and local governments, with the primary intent of determining the scope of cleanup. It ends with reoccupation of the evacuated zone, an indication that the emergency is over and you are entering the final cleanup phase.

Federal agencies

Depending on the style of the event, there can be from six to a dozen or more federal coordinators on scene, representing as many agencies. There may be additional specialists in air, water, and solid waste. As long as the spill involves waters of the United States, they will always be under the direction of a *predesignated* OSC and will be functioning under the edicts of the 1510 plan. You as a local official may be close to a specific member of the RRT because your job relates to his or her federal job. Work closely with this person and other RRT members to ensure that your views are clearly heard by the RRT. You actually have a triple responsibility in that you must also work closely with both the LOSC and your counterpart on the state team. For example, FEMA, state civil defense representatives, and local civil defense officials must work together to consolidate specific views and needs, but the voice speaking to the spillor should now be that of the federal OSC. This OSC has arrived at a point of view and has developed instructions for the spillor by listening to the RRT. This same concept extends to every official on-scene, so that all interests have a voice in every decision made and passed on to the spillor for action.

The Environment Protection Agency (EPA) If this is an inland spill, the OSC will be an official predesignated by EPA. If coastal, the OSC will be from the Coast Guard. For the purpose of illustration in this chapter, the OSC will be from EPA. The OSC will be the voice of the federal government and will also serve as the agent of the RRT. Since he or she basically works with the advice and aid of the RRT, this person will be your voice. The 1510 plan allows the OSC much freedom and flexibility, but the *wise* OSC will work closely with the RRT on every major decision. The OSC function is briefly outlined in Chapter 2, and the complete version is in the 1510 plan. The presiding officer ("chair") of the RRT is a predesignated official from the OSC's agency and coordinates all information available to the OSC. The wise chair will appoint officials from the state and local agencies to cochair. If they have not been predesignated, the LOSC and SOSC can serve on the RRT or appoint others to represent them there. EPA may also send officials from media programs such as air, solid waste, and drinking water. The presiding officer, through the RRT during the initial meeting, must assign tasks to the various groups, preferably in their respective specialty areas. Most assigned tasks are a reaffirmation of duties already vested. This mechanism simply makes sure nothing falls through the cracks and it provides a tremendous endorsement of what you are already doing under your various authorities.

The Coast Guard The Coast Guard will be serving the OSC and the RRT in such areas as contractor management, communications, and cleanup methodology. EPA, of course, would serve the Coast Guard OSC as environmental consultant during coastal spills.

The EPA Emergency Response Team (ERT) This is a specialty team (usually one to three people) designed to aid the OSC and RRT in scientific areas.

The Department of Interior (Fish and Wildlife) Through their pollution response coordinator, information is furnished on fish, wildlife, and endangered species.

The Department of Defense (DOD) The DOD may have a number of agencies represented on-scene but only one DOD representative on the RRT. On-scene there could be the Army Reserve in support of the OSC; the Air Force or Navy furnishing air observation or critical overflights; the U.S. Corps of Engineers (COE) furnishing a temporary water supply; or the EOD (demolition specialists), handling explosive materials or exploding the tank car that the RRT has determined must be exploded. Any one or all of these must work through the DOD representative in servicing the needs of the OSC and the RRT.

Federal Emergency Management Agency (FEMA) Coordination is the key here. A well-run cleanup and recovery operation is one highlighted by maximum local input and continual liaison between local, state, and federal agencies. FEMA is ideal for this task.

Department of Commerce (National Oceanographic and Atmospheric Administration, NOAA) Through NOAA's scientific support coordination representative, the research and academic communities can be involved in critical events. In this way, new and innovative scientific techniques can be made available and used when appropriate. NOAA has always assisted with weather information.

National Transportation and Safety Board (NTSB) and the FBI The need for investigation is very important. If you work through the OSC (by way of your participation on the RRT), your priorities will be acknowledged. With the exception of emergencies involving life or death or situations which will extend the evacuation unreasonably, the OSC will make every effort to avoid moving anything until you have completed your inspection. While at this writing the NTSB has declined membership in the National Response Team, investigators have shown an inclination toward participating in RRT meetings on-scene. The FBI, of course, participates through the Department of Justice which is a member of the NRT.

Department of Health and Human Services Through HHS's national Center for Disease Control (CDC) in Atlanta, medical advice will be available 24 hours a day, nationwide. This advice will focus on chronic and acute situations in the area of medical toxicology.

Poison control centers At various hospitals in every large city, there is a 24-hour poison control team. Team personnel will assist in emergency medical problems, e.g., analyzing symptoms when the causative chemical is unknown.

Others In certain areas of the country such as the Tennessee Valley and the Ohio River Basin, authorities such as TVA and/or Commissions such as the Ohio River Sanitation Commission are members of the RRT because of their specific knowledge of and interest in that geographical area. They possess vital background information on water quality. They also have press and public contacts, specialized equipment, and communication facilities; and they are keenly interested in helping.

If extremely large areas are evacuated, if much destruction or closing of industries takes place, and if the need for massive federal aid becomes obvious, an accident could evolve to the presidential declaration stage. FEMA would then be alerted and a whole new style of federal involvement set in motion. At this time, a federal coordinating official (FCO) would be sent to the area, and federal and state agencies would be given mission assignments to quantify damage and disburse federal funds. The cleanup mission under the RRT and OSC would continue intact. The RRT would be functioning as a distinct entity but would also become a part of the entire exercise under the Federal Disaster Relief Act. Nothing really changes except that there is additional work for agencies with mission assignments.

State agencies

Civil Defense Organization A working partnership is formed by FEMA, the local civil defense director, and the SOSC (who may be a civil defense official). As in phase 1, coordination is a principal role.

National Guard and/or Army Reserve The layout and management of staging or rest areas is vital to the operation. Tents, cots, fans or heaters, lights, etc., are too often taken for granted. There may be additional roles, but work with the LOSC to ensure best use of your resources.

State On-Scene Coordinator (SOSC) As a member of the RRT (perhaps in a cochairing role) your function should be to coordinate all state activities. The federal OSC views you as a representative of the governor. Therefore your voice on the RRT is considered to be that of safety, public health and welfare, and all phases of pollution control.

State Pollution Control Authority Many states assign the SOSC role to the pollution control agency. Most of the people monitoring and supervising air, water wells, domestic water-treatment plants, stream pollution, soil evaluation, and ultimate disposal are personnel of this agency. Phases 2 and 3 are largely efforts involving these kinds of expertise. This role begins to develop the first day and may last for weeks. Long-term monitoring may involve a year or more. Because of the complexity of this role, you must work with your federal counterpart during phase 2. In addition, you must communicate all your activities to the OSC and LOSC through your SOSC.

State's Attorney or State Bureau of Investigation The same concept that applies to federal investigators would apply to you. Simply work through the SOSC to point up your priorities and needs.

Local agencies

Somewhat bewildered by all of this help, you are concerned about your role in phase 2. Despite the feeling at times that you have been taken out of the game, you are still involved in various degrees. *Remember,* the local need is always the chief cleanup criterion.

Civil Defense Organization Your role continues throughout phase 2.

Firefighting Agency and Fire Marshal This role begins to fade during phase 2 in terms of resource and equipment requirements. This is a matter of judgment, but within several days after the accident, the probability of fire and explosion should be reduced to the extent that you can begin to withdraw some of your equipment. There may be a need, however, for at least one unit at the command post or in the staging area until the end of phase 2.

Sheriff and Local and State Police (Highway Patrol, State Troopers) The roadblocks will, of course, require continual operation, and the evacuation area will have to be patrolled until the end of phase 2. However, if the conditions are such that the evacuation area can be gradually reduced, you may expect relief in resource demands. The LOSC will need your help in reoccupation efforts.

County Commissioner, Mayor, or County Judge Your role now becomes one of keeping your community informed and of reestablishing confidence in the area and its future uses. The emergency is changing into a long-term cleanup with state and federal officials playing larger roles. The community as a whole needs to know that this is not an indication of failure on the part of local efforts, but rather the full utilization of the services and expertise of specialists in this unique business. As an example, when the water-supply system is declared safe, you together with the three principals in cleanup (OSC, LOSC, and SOSC) should, publicize the fact, via radio, television, and press releases, the fact that the system is open and safe. It is a good idea to hold a public meeting at the end of phase 2. Let the people air their frustrations.

Spillor and Technical Assist Groups As cleanup begins to develop, the spillor and the expert groups on specific chemicals must continue to work, using the OSC's instructions as the blueprint. Many times the spillor will ask for and receive on-site advice from groups with special competence concerning certain chemicals. This effort should be coordinated with the RRT so that such advice can be considered in light of all the advice being given by others. This is *critical.*

The Cleanup Contractor or Work Force As previously stated, one part of the spillor's responsibility under the federal law is *adequate* cleanup. (The RRT will usually assess this situation.) It may involve excavation and disposal of contaminated soil, protection of streams and water supplies, removal and *proper* disposal of liquid contaminants, the patching of tanks, rerailing cars or removing vehicles, or removing and disposing of debris. Many events necessitate more than one contractor or work force. The spillor may use its own resources, but if the RRT and OSC deem the effort inadequate, the federal government may take over the cleanup and hire its own forces or fund those currently at work. Of course, there will be subsequent legal action to recover these funds plus exceptional expenses. Not much physical work in terms of cleanup actually begins until phase 2.

Red Cross and Salvation Army Your role will continue throughout phase 2.

EMT Your role will also continue throughout phase 2, during which you may be able to reduce your resources. Once again, it's a matter of judgment.

Phase 3

Usually starting somewhere between the second and sixth day of the event and lasting until the area is clean, this phase is the final cleanup that will provide long-term protection to the public and environment. The area is no longer evacuated when this final phase begins.

Federal agencies

The numbers of federal officials are sharply reduced during this phase. Don't be confused; they have not abandoned their effort. Much of their work can now be done at the home office, and their input can be given directly to the OSC. The OSC remains and now will coordinate the smaller, but just as effective, RRT. The full RRT can always be reactivated for such matters as reviewing progress and/or proclaiming that the area is clean and the exercise completed.

EPA The EPA is now represented by the OSC (the presiding officer of the RRT has departed), the ERT, and in some cases a solid waste and/or drinking water specialist. Often these specialists can work effectively out of their home office(s).

The Coast Guard The strike team generally remains throughout the exercise and leaves with the OSC.

DOI (Fish and Wildlife) This agency has probably departed for the home office, and like other departed RRT members, will be kept informed by periodic telegrams referred to as *polreps* (pollution reports), or *sitreps* (situation reports).

DOD With the exception of the COE (which could be doing such tasks as furnishing a temporary drinking water supply), this agency has departed.

Others The following have gone home but are still involved:

Defense Civil Preparedness
Department of Commerce
National Transportation and Safety Board and the FBI
Department of Health and Human Services (CDC)
Poison control centers
All others

State agencies

The SOSC and the Pollution Control Authority Much remains to be done by these officials in conjunction with the OSC and the strike team. Stream and soil monitoring may last for weeks before the site is clean to the point that it is generally usable and will not leach pollutants beyond acceptable levels into the streams. The state solid waste official must, in conjunction with EPA, locate an acceptable land disposal site. The state air official, in conjunction with EPA, must find a location for the destruction (incineration) of unreclaimable liquids. As the work progresses toward completion, the full RRT may be reassembled to determine if the site requires a quarantine and, if so, for how long. If perimeter wells and long-term monitoring of stream and/or drinking water are necessary, questions about how much monitoring, for how long, and where may also need discussion by the RRT.

Others The following have gone home but are still involved:

Civil defense representatives
National Guard and/or Army Reserves
State's attorney or state bureau of investigation

Local agencies

After the area is reoccupied and the cleanup is well under way, your responsibilities on-scene diminish. The OSC will be available to keep each agency informed, and you will be asked for permissions and advice during final cleanup. When the RRT is activated to evaluate when to cease the operation, your presence and full participation will be necessary.

The Spillor Your work with the OSC continues. Since all incidental expenses relating to the accident fall on you, you need to set up a method of managing claims for damage. Such matters as payment of motel bills for evacuated persons (when necessary) must be tended to immediately.

The Cleanup Contractor Physical work, of course, will continue *under the direction of your employer, the spillor.* The OSC will make the various governments' requirements known at all times to the spillor.

Conclusion

At first glance, many of you may feel that the role outlined for you above is shallow and doesn't include all of your authority in your current position. Realistically, is all of your authority really appropriate? That can only be understood and evaluated by you after you read and thoroughly appreciate every other role. As an example of evaluating your general authority versus your role in the hazardous substance accident, let's say you are a state trooper manning a roadblock. The OSC drives up, informs you that she is the OSC, shows authentic identification, and says she must enter the evacuated area. You detain her, per your state police powers, based on safety. Is this reasonable? Are you technically responsible for her safety? You can arrest her for failing to obey an order, etc., etc., but you must consider her duty and authority as well as yours. If you have read Chapter 2, Section 2-1, it is obvious that in terms of federal law she is responsible for the safety of the whole exercise. The author's advice is, let her go. She is traveling under legal colors, and you have cautioned her. This is an excellent example of why we must all know each other's responsibilities in order to efficiently manage the episode.

Finally, don't be upset if a toe gets stepped on to some extent. Toes are always exposed in tight quarters. When someone in authority appears to be encroaching, 99.9 percent of the time it is not intentional. Coordinated events of any kind will always have areas of overlap. The alternative which would eliminate overlap is the one-person-in-charge concept. By now this concept should be recognized as unrealistic for the events we are discussing.

7-3 PERSONNEL SAFETY AND LIABILITIES

Safety is difficult to write about. It has been defined as *the condition of being safe from undergoing or causing hurt, injury, or loss.* Today there is an entire federal government agency charged with enforcing the *conditions* of safety. Although the Occupational Safety and Health Administration (OSHA) is active mostly in the area of working conditions, it is showing a growing concern for field safety at emergencies. The subject of safety involves an entire field of law and terms such as *assumption of risk, duty, proximate cause, res ipsa loquitur, strict liability, contributory negligence, respondeat superior, agency,* and many others. It is not necessary or even reasonable to expect the average person involved in spill response to retain all those words, let alone the legal concepts they may describe. But be aware that today's safety is complex and worthy of study.

Much of what we will discuss here will involve the word *duty.* Questions arise such as: What is your duty? Is it specific? If so, what is the significance of failure to perform, and what are the consequences of properly performing the duty and undergoing or causing injury or hurt?

Let's look at some current legal concepts in this area. Keep in mind that the following examples are used to show general trends in the law and are not offered as legal advice.

Lay Persons

Lay persons generally have no official duty to act, but once they begin to act, they should not abandon the effort. Also, any effort attempted must not be made negligently. As an example, Joe witnesses Bill being crushed beneath a truck wheel as the result of an accident. A jack is near by, but in fear, Joe watches Bill die. This may sound cruel, but there is probably no legal action for Bill's heirs. Joe had no *duty* to act. Let's say Joe does act. He grabs the jack and tries desperately to lift the truck, but soon tiring, he throws the jack handle down and walks off. This abandonment may give rise to a legal action, depending on circumstances. Taking this one more step, let's say Joe attempts to help but negligently injures Bill more than if he had waited to allow a lift truck to remove the wheel. Joe may be liable here. The point is: act if you must, but do not be negligent—i.e., be reasonable.

Duty-Bound Officials

Those with a duty to act are in an entirely different arena. No duty can require the sacrifice of your life or that of another. However, specific response to certain situations may be a part of your job. Your failure to act could be translated into negligence and become cause for legal action. What is your duty? You need to know this specifically, so ask your counsel (city or county attorney, state's attorney, or your regional counsel). Be specific; ask what your agency relationship is. (An *agency* in law is a relationship whereby one party, called an agent, is *authorized* to represent the other party, called a principal, in dealings with third parties.) Find out in no uncertain terms if your typical actions in responding to an accident are duly authorized by your organization. Find out if you *are* their agent, and if so, whether your judgments transfer to them for liability purposes. You may be surprised at the answer.

In governmental groups, supervisors are becoming increasingly anxious as their employees perform their duties in this new area of hazardous substances. During a 1978 accident involving the spilling of a number of toxic chemicals, a state official went to the scene and retrieved a number of samples for analysis (as he had been doing for several years). Several days after returning to his office, he became ill and reported this to his supervisor. The supervisor immediately wrote the man an official letter of reprimand, alleging "poor safety practices." Was the supervisor's action justifiable? It depends on several factors. Did the agency have a safety policy with specific parameters, one or more of which the employee violated? Was the official an agent acting for his principal? If not, what is the basis for his duty to gather the samples? Most governmental officials are loyal to their organizations and do what they perceive to be their duty automatically and without questioning the legal ramifications. They also labor under the mistaken belief that to fail to do this duty or to argue about it is insubordination.

Today we are witnessing a growing concern about the legal questions involved with safety. More and more official edicts are circulated to the worker, saying, "Do your duty but do it safely," or "This organization is safety-oriented. Anyone violating safety rules will be dealt with accordingly." What does all this mean in the context of accident response?

Classical Safety

"Safety in the workshop" has evolved over many years to a virtual science. The wearing of safety boots, gloves, goggles, breathing masks, the periodic physicals, etc., are built into essentially every function in the workplace. Time and motion studies and output functions embrace safety at every step. Equipment is designed with classical safety concepts in mind.

At the scene of the accident, classical safety can be established immediately. Evacuation, road blocks, and use of specialized personal gear by officials who must be near the cleanup zone for an indeterminate length of time are well-developed techniques. It is relatively easy, then, to implement safety procedures for these activities and to determine whether the employee is acting properly. Firefighters, members of National Guard and the civil defense organization, state troopers, and sheriff's personnel are all involved daily in duties that involve classical safety. Many of the techniques utilized at the typical wreck, fire, or riot will apply at the hazardous substances scene, but the duty is not nearly so clear. Do you really have to hose down that burning car of vinyl chloride (the one next to the car of metallic sodium)? Do you really have to get the bodies out of the chemical warehouse *now?* Do you *have* to drag that person from his or her home? We begin to see distinctions in duty that may warrant a whole new concept of safety.

Emergency Safety

When accidents occur, they are extremely dynamic with respect to duty. Each accident involving hazardous materials is different, and decisions involving life and death are made in a heartbeat. The "reasonable man" so useful in law to quantify negligence is a new person in these events. It is much more difficult in such situations to clearly determine what is *reasonable*. Because judgments are so difficult and time is so short, the official making the on-scene decisions and those carrying out the orders simply cannot worry about classical safety or legal consequences, and many times mistakes are made. But in 12 years the author has seen little error that was substantially more significant than the probable result had no action been taken at all. And on only two occasions in the more than 500 spills attended has the author seen a bona fide safety official (in charge of the safety of personnel for the agency) on-scene. Only after agency safety personnel have come on-scene and evaluated problems from that perspective are they adequately prepared to design a program that will describe your duty, limiting both your liability and that of the group you represent.

There is also that unique and hybrid group that does the physical work—removing debris, uprighting the truck, rerailing the railroad cars, or patching the tank. Safety here is a most difficult issue. Are we going to tell a highly qualified worker what equipment must be worn while placing 400 pounds (181 kg) of TNT to extinguish the oil well fire? Or when we request a demolition specialist to place plastic explosives on a tank car to ignite and burn it, are we going to dictate the location of the backup crew or the placement of the charge? We are talking about risks and risk analysis at this point. We have all seen these things—the official sliding down the wrecked tank car of aminotoluene, attempting to close the leaky valve which is dripping on a house below, or people not wearing rubberized suits and air tanks while working in the smoldering warehouse. Do we order them to put on the equipment? If so, what is our position when they get overheated, pass out, and injure themselves? If we order the man off the car and some worker is injured by the leak, what is our liability? Some people in high places in government have recently observed that perhaps government shouldn't be involved. That is one answer but it is not an acceptable one. The Congress, state legislatures, and local governments have issued the response laws, and they will be enforced, properly or improperly.

Safety from the Management Perspective

The title of this book, *Managing Hazardous Substances Accidents*, suggests the answer to the emergency safety dilemma. *Managing* means directing, coordinating; it has nothing to do with "hands-on" work. During all phases of the work, from the impact until final cleanup, managers need spend only minimal time in the impact area. Immediately after impact, only fire crews should be near the accident. A backup fire team and an emergency medical unit should be located within a 1- to 2-minute response time, but all spare equipment, supervisors, and others should be located at least one to several miles away. Evacuation teams should begin as close to impact as possible and move outward. Once the area is stabilized, the entire scene should be cleared. A small evaluation team consisting of two air specialists (with at least an explosion meter, oxygen analyzer, and an air-sampler kit), a fire specialist, and two helpers should then enter the area. The time lag should be 2 to 6 hours, depending on the size and amounts of fire and gas emissions. Beyond that inspection, only minimal work crews and an occasional visit by specialty experts and the OSC are necessary. Even when the area is stabilized, and what appears to be normal cleanup has begun, impact area attendance should be minimized. No one should assume that a violent explosion cannot occur, even in the final stages of cleanup. We need only remember the staggering price paid at Waverly, Tennessee. There are times when investigative officials must go on-scene—and don't forget the press. The National Transportation Safety Board, the FBI, and the state's attorney have a vested interest and must be allowed to investigate before anything is moved, if at all possible. The OSC, LOSC, and SOSC must use judgment in these cases, and the best way to handle the press is to assemble them and carry them in as a group. This should be done as soon as possible and repeated at least daily. But remember, the spillor has prime liability and rights, and should have the last say. How close to the impact area the press should go is again a matter of judgment; during phase 2, however, 500 feet (152 m) is adequate with the cameras available today. Of course, no one should be in the area during phase 1.

Equipment

No one (press included) should go near the accident without protective gear. Always look at the shoes of casual observers: High heels and sandals are *out,* period!

There are a number of companies in this country that make safety equipment. Figures 7-1 through 7-8 show some of the gear that is in frequent use today. Generally, each type of breathing apparatus has a specific use, and probably the most interesting piece of breathing gear is the five-minute oxygen escape pack.

Consider your role and classical safety if you are a manager, official, sheriff, civil defense worker, OSC, LOSC, SOSC, press representative, or industrial official: How close do you really need to be and for how long? Perhaps until that rare, close-proximity inspection, you need only carry an escape mask or a small breathing mask. If so, carry it with you everywhere. In your car, hang it on the rear-view mirror, or put it on *top* of all your equipment in the front seat. If your duty requires longer on-scene time, then wear appropriate equipment. Firefighters, chemical teams, and—in the early stages—the National Guard, sheriff, and EMT personnel fit this category. If you are responsible for these groups of people, then your duty is obviously to see that they are trained, *that they practice,* and that they have the *best* equipment money can buy. Your failure to do any of this could not only be construed as a breach of your duty, but could cause confusion as to what their duty requirement really is. Finally, if you are that special person who has to put his or her hands

Fig. 7-1 Organic canister with mask.

on the debris, remove the bung, or patch the tank, this writer simply is not qualified to do more than make generalized observations. Have the best equipment, and either use it at all times or keep it near. If you have to patch the car or drive the bulldozer that turns the chlorine car over to dump it, there is only a handful of people in the world capable of instructing you. But someone sent you there, gave you the duty, and is concerned for your safety. If you can be just as safe wearing your equipment, wear it! Managers must, on the other hand, remember that what appears to be a totally unsafe condition may be, in fact, the *only way*. At that point, the act may be reasonable and your contrary instruction totally unreasonable, even if you are talking classical

Fig. 7-2 Organic filter without mask.

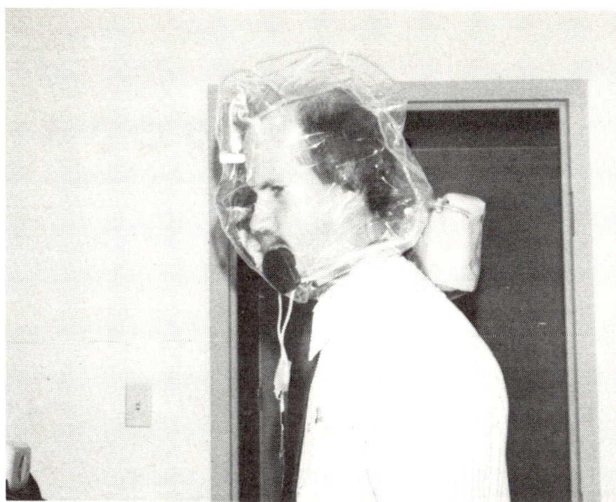

Fig. 7-3 Five-minute oxygen escape pack.

safety. The man reaching between the two cars may not be wearing an air tank because its weight and restriction on movement would make the task a deadly one. He may have taken his rubber suit off because it is so hot he fears fainting and sudden death. There will always be risks; our job is to minimize them. To this end, we must remember several things:

1 Use only well-trained experts in this area. Check their credentials. Don't accept colorful brochures claiming expertise. The RRT will always have a method of checking credentials.

2 Watch for recklessness. Don't accept it, but be sure to carefully assess what you see before you decide it is reckless.

Fig. 7-4 Full protective suit with oxygen (air) tank.

Fig. 7-5 Military-type mask with organic filter, in use on a hazardous dump site.

3 "Never tell the surgeon how to sew up the cut." You may decide that the present risk is so great that no one should proceed. This is fine. But at some point someone will have to proceed, and must be allowed to use the needed expertise.

4 Don't wait until after the fact to criticize the specialist. If you see a reckless situation, report it *then*. Contact the OSC; the RRT and spillor will be informed and the situation halted. This takes only seconds by radio.

Fig. 7-6 An oxygen system that filters and regenerates respired oxygen.

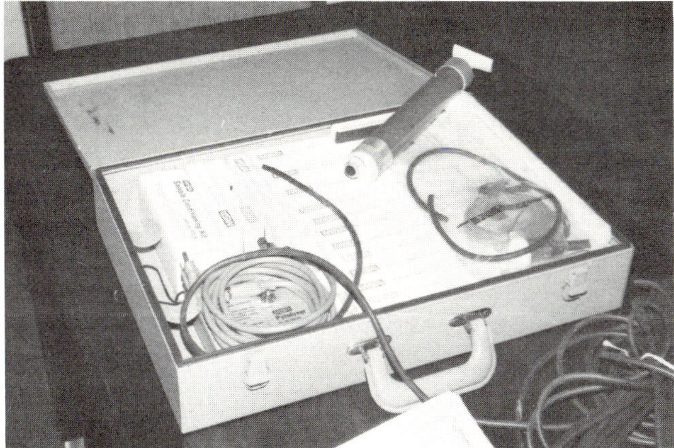

Fig. 7-7 A simple air-monitoring kit.

7-4 EVACUATION

Evacuation is the necessary evil of hazardous substance episodes. No one can argue the need, but the decisions regarding method, accommodations, and length of time are critical. Deaths have been recorded that were chargeable only to the fact that the evacuation occurred. To appreciate the problem, all you have to do is select a typical urban or suburban area 1 mile square and evaluate the people and social contingencies in that area. Involved are:

Fig. 7-8 A trained air-monitoring specialist at work.

1 The sick (physically and mentally)
2 Those on continual medication
3 The apprehension of family separation
4 The elderly
5 Valuable possessions
6 Pets
7 Livestock
8 Tasks that will be left undone

Your education in spill management will never be complete until you have visited an evacuation shelter and talked with the people directly affected. An understanding of how they perceive what has happened to them is invaluable. Most people are not bitter; they are apprehensive, afraid, uncomfortable, and—at times—alone. They worry much more about other people and things than about their own plight. The heart patient, the asthmatic, and the epileptic will draw unbelievable concern from their kin. People have to be arrested for running roadblocks to obtain medication for a friend who *had* to have *that* medicine. They also worry about their possessions, some of which may be worth little in the marketplace but are of much greater value to their owners. Is the oven on or the window up? These are problems that can drive normal people to do strange and risky things. Possessions and house are life itself for the elderly. People 70 years old are not interested in a discussion about how they can eventually recover economically.

And the Yorkshire terrier left behind at the elderly lady's house is not just her pet, it's her companion. The same thing applies to the farmer's old bluetick hound or his wife's milk cow or Persian cat. Once the sick have been accommodated, and those who are apprehensive about the well-being of kin have been soothed and settle down, the issue of animals is without question of prime importance. Who is going to feed and water them? There is simply nothing in any of our laws—federal, state, or local—that provides specifically for this, yet people will risk arrest or danger to see to it.

In 1979 at Crestview, Florida, I witnessed a touching event. Because of a very serious train wreck, people were evacuated from their homes 5½ days. Unnoticed by everyone except those at the staging area were a number of cats and dogs, scattered throughout the evacuated area. Dogs and cats will typically stay in the vicinity of their homes, even when they are vacant. I have seen such animals starve at the deserted doorstep. During the third day of this particular event, I noticed a rather large quantity of dog and cat food in the rear of the EPA air specialist's car. When I asked about it, I was told that during his air-monitoring rounds, the young man had been feeding the dogs and cats with food purchased from his own pocket (about $10–$15 per day). In fact, unknown to anyone, he had been succoring animals since the chlorine accident at Youngstown, Florida, in 1978. But this person was a well-trained

Fig. 7-9 Tending the animals during an evacuation.

specialist, and because of unique knowledge and equipment was able to act in safety. Later, at a Senate hearing in downtown Crestview, a group of people who had been evacuated to the local National Guard Armory approached me. They had two questions: what could they do about their pets and how long were they to be away from their homes? When I told them what the young man was doing, one elderly couple sat down and cried.—A beautiful touch to an otherwise tragic event.

Before undertaking similar acts, however, please coordinate with the OSC. Every effort will be made to have concerned evacuees accompanied by a specialist and, of course, timing must be carefully considered (Figure 7-9).

The technical aspects of evacuation are as difficult as the social issues. The critical question will always be: How big an area should be evacuated? How long evacuation will last will naturally depend on how competently the first phase of cleanup is managed.

Within minutes of the accident, the first officials arrive on or near the scene. The first order of business is to get the immediate area evacuated. The people involved here require little urging, but simply a direction in which to go. If fire is a big problem, perimeter cooling can begin simultaneously with initial evacuation. Caution! Don't get too close. There is little you can save on-scene with water; the best you can hope for is explosion control. Initial fire-control efforts should always be defensive. Be ready to retreat, and have your equipment arranged in withdrawal positions. Get EMT units into the area as quickly as possible. Civil defense workers, sheriff, local police, and spillor officials are to begin the next stage of evacuation immediately. Use bullhorns or whatever is available, and set up teams moving in concentric circles. Have one team move clockwise, the next counterclockwise. The theory is that the overlapping amplified warning may prewarn those in the next block before the team arrives. Finally, have follow-up teams moving in the same pattern, closing and locking doors, checking ovens, windows, lights, etc. If the situation is too volatile, move back. You can continue later when you have received proper equipment and additional help. Don't forget to tell everyone where to go. Pick out a well-known spot (not too far away, since some may be walking), and make sure every announcement relays this location to the evacuees. Immediately send one of your staff members to receive them, and get ready for the Red Cross and Salvation Army to begin sheltering them.

How far do we evacuate initially? This is always a favorite discussion for "Monday morning quarterbacks," but a 1-mile radius is a reasonable goal to start with. Experience has shown that considering the resources needed, the desire not to traumatize people unnecessarily, and the dynamics of most chemical events, this is adequate as an emergency effort. Of course each accident is different. The chemicals, their mixing capabilities, the winds, explosions, and flying debris are all potentially different. Many times the prevailing surface winds and the gases emitted are such that the evacuated area will be egg-shaped. If the smells are still noxious at 1 mile, then extend the area. Hopefully, after these first few hours you can fall back and regroup. Once the state and federal people arrive, there should be scientific instruments available to help evaluate the evacuation area. Remember, evacuate as you feel necessary, but be as conservative as possible. And if air-monitoring readings will allow even partial reoccupation, give it serious consideration.

When the area is evacuated and secure, roving patrols (with adequate breathing equipment) should continually move throughout the area, keeping a sharp eye for curiosity seekers, looters, and people going back for something they forgot.

Reoccupation is a happy time, but it must be done with some formality. Prior to leaving the shelters, *everyone* should be briefed as to what happened and where and when to file claims they may have for any and all damages. The spillor should be involved in this meeting. Last of all, everyone should be warned that cleanup is continuing on-scene and that they must stay out of the cleanup area. Individuals who have suffered specific damage such as contamination of water wells, gardens, etc., must be instructed individually as to what they can or cannot do.

7-5 CROWD CONTROL

Crowd control involves many factors and all kinds of people, including officials. Perhaps it can be viewed as a management concept that involves regulating all movement of people on-scene and at the perimeter command posts. The following are a few of the unfortunate incidents I have witnessed or heard about over the years:

1 A local official, accompanied by his 12-year-old son (neither with air masks) retrieved a body from an accident site while the facility that emitted the original death cloud was still leaking and in the same position as when it released that cloud.

2 At a similar incident, a federal official rode around the evacuated area in an official car with his young daughter beside him. Both had only minimum safety equipment.

3 A lawyer crashed his vehicle into a roadblock, breaking the leg of a sheriff's deputy.

4 A distraught resident slugged a deputy sheriff and a state trooper at a roadblock.

5 A member of the press, shoes and camera in hand, clawed a path up a hill inside a roadblock just to get a few pictures.

6 A group of teenagers were talking and smoking cigarettes inside a roadblock which was protecting a large gasoline spill into a small stream. A match was thrown into the stream. It ignited the gasoline, which quickly burned for a mile upstream, nearly killing the teenagers, the OSC, and several workers.

7 Cleanup officials were smoking cigarettes while standing ankle deep in diesel fuel.

All of this is related to crowd control. Officials must exhibit self-control themselves as they attempt to control others.

The best mechanism for controlling those evacuated is keeping them informed. Give a detailed briefing at least twice a day. There will always be a few people who *must* enter the evacuated area. While this activity has to be held to a minimum, it may be necessary to prevent a more serious incident. The shelter manager can listen to such requests, and, if they are legitimate, call the LOSC to request permission. If the LOSC agrees, the person can be taken to the roadblock. If the OSC feels that the timing is right, i.e., nothing risky is going on and a vehicle is available, then perhaps a deputy or police officer will act as escort. Proper equipment should be taken and a record made of the trip for legal reasons. For the same reasons, the escorting official should be a sheriff's deputy, state trooper, or local police officer.

The pressure at roadblocks is tremendous. Make no mistake about it, the people who operate these are truly heroes. Their duty is somewhat confusing, as is their authority. They are frequently abused by citizens and officials alike, and they are also frequently injured. As a general rule, local people who are inconvenienced by a roadblock will exhibit the following pattern of behavior:

Day 1–2: They will be curious, but cordial and understanding.

Day 3: They will ask how cleanup is going, why they can't use the road (the accident is a mile away, and this road cuts 7 miles off their route to work), and whether people are really working on-scene.

Day 4: Some individuals get testy. Remarks are made; tempers flare.

Day 5: Some citizens will use physical force.

Add to this the dozens of visitors, officials, and others who have "compelling" reasons to go on-scene, and you have the makings of a real problem.

You need some means of control; require that no one may go on-scene without signing in and out; in this way, a continuous accounting of people can be maintained. Also, insist that only the people who are necessary should go on-scene. By way of suggestion:

1 At the first RRT meeting, the full team—local, state, and federal—should compile a list of all those who have a real need to be on-scene. These people should wear a colored tag as a permanent pass, but must still sign in and out. Among them will be the OSC, SOSC, LOSC, two or three spillor officials, the cleanup crew, civil defense officials, fire officials, and air-monitoring specialists.

2 Others who develop a need to go on-scene on any particular day should go to the command post and have the OSC issue a pass of a different color, good for that day only. The individuals must also sign in and out. In this group will be scientists and relevant experts, water specialists, NTSB, FBI agents, and state investigators.

3 Emergency passes good for 1 hour on any day could be still a different color and must be issued by the OSC. Holders of such passes again must sign in and out. This group would include VIPs, the press, and evacuees.

Overflights should be prohibited except by express permission of the OSC in conjunction with the FAA.

chapter

EIGHT

Cleanup Technology

At the end of what we have called phase 1, we must plan phases 2 and 3 by using the various management concepts of accident response. Undoubtedly many of the activities in phase 1 will have substantial impact on these later phases. It would be nice if we had done nothing in the early moments of the episode that would be troublesome later, but it simply doesn't work that way. The most frequently discussed problem is the excessive use or misuse of firefighting water during the initial stages. Equally disastrous results can be achieved by simply mixing the wrong chemicals or committing the team to a cleanup method that later must be totally changed or abandoned.

As previously mentioned, the technology in hazardous substance accident response and management lags considerably behind our needs. Specialized equipment is still on the drawing boards, and cleanup techniques are largely underdeveloped. The few cleanup contractors competent in the area of hazardous substances accidents are in most cases fabricating their own equipment to fit the exotic requirements specified for them.

Because of these considerations and the fact that no two incidents are the same, there are no fixed or "school" solutions to any of these episodes. However, the combining of existing components into a tailored package may very well represent the optimum solution to a specific event. Usefulness of these components is a subject that must be explored.

The various technical applications discussed in this chapter will appear to lack engineering excellence or architectural flair; nevertheless review them carefully, noting the limitations and capabilities of each. Sometime, somewhere, some or all of the principles outlined may be an aid in a dynamic situation. And don't be surprised to find that the underflow dam shown in Figure 8-1 is a beautiful application of Bernoulli's theorem.

Fig. 8-1 A small but effective underflow dam.

In 1738 Daniel Bernoulli presented his famous energy equation depicting the dynamics of fluid flow:

$$\frac{P_1}{w} + Z_1 + \frac{v_1^2}{2\mathbf{g}} = \frac{P_2}{w} + Z_2 + \frac{v_2^2}{2\mathbf{g}}$$

where

P_1 and P_2 = fluid pressure
v_1 and v_2 = velocity of flow
Z_1 and Z_2 = vertical height of flow (liquid elevations)
w = mass density of fluid
$\mathbf{g}$ = accleration due to gravity

This equation is simply an energy balance between two distinct points in a frictionless, incompressible fluid. If we know the pipe size and the required flow, we can calculate velocities, pressures, liquid elevations, and pipe invert elevations, or we can place the pipe in a dam and manipulate the outfall end by hand or foot until the pond level is stable (adding pipes as necessary). When we do the latter, we have constructed a crude but effective underflow dam and have balanced the equation without even knowing the concept involved. There is a valuable point here. The dynamics of chemical emergencies require a unique blend of technical knowledge and horse sense. There is never time for long-range planning, well-articulated methods, or philosophical discussions. Time is critical! Therefore, the approach used may not be pretty, but it is technically sound. The hardware and equipment employed in cleanup may look more like something from the farm toolshed than the activated-carbon system it really is. The question is: Does it work?

Many of the applications described below may not work in events similar to those during which they originated. Field chemistry, for example, cannot always be approximated in the laboratory. A classical example is the mixture of concentrated acids and alkaline compounds. While reviewing the following cleanup concepts, remember that they are generalizations that must be evaluated by you or your team as to their applicability to specific problems.

8-1 CONTAINMENT

Land Spills

Containment

Without question, the idea of containing spilled chemicals in the smallest area or device possible and as close to the source as practical will keynote most events. Confining the danger and/or pollutant always pays dividends in terms of money, health, and welfare. However, the philosophy of containment includes certain notes of caution. In considering containment you must:

1 Assess the proximity of people to the containment area.

2 Make some judgment as to whether the chemical is more dangerous in volume than if it is spread over a large area. For example, workers engaged in containing an oxygen inhibitor like aminotoluene must not breathe it or get the compound on their bodies. Consequently, containment of this chemical may cause more problems than would arise from permitting it to spread. The issue here is danger, not environment.

3 Question the security of the containment area. Is it good enough? Is it practical?

Technical questions concerning containment usually have obvious answers, and only rarely will a situation arise where containment is not favored.

Methods of containment are numerous and to a large degree involve the instincts and innovativeness of the first responders. Many types of containment "apparatus" are available:

1 Dikes that afford direct containment

2 Dams that plug drainage swales or ditches

3 Natural topography

4 Excavated sumps

5 Trenches

6 Ponds

7 Streams

8 Temporary patching of the source, which may include pushing a mound of dirt on top of the leaking tank.

All methods have limitations that must be considered, but those that are most difficult and should be studied with great care involve surface-water containment. The use of a portion of a stream or a natural pond for impounding a chemical and expediting cleanup is practical only in dire emergencies.

Isolation

Another almost instinctive reaction of first responders should be the separation and isolation of individual chemicals. If the capability exists, this is an immediate must. There are numerous quick and easy methods of keeping spilled liquid chemicals from mixing. Small windrows threaded through the area, hastily excavated pits, and soil mounded over a tank or against the wall of a tank are examples. In soft soils a bulldozer or other piece of heavy equipment can often be operated in such a way that the track print will become a gravity conduit to pull like chemicals together. Once again certain cautions should be noted:

1 Worker exposure is maximum, therefore body protection is critical.

2 Debris must be kept clear of pools of liquids.

3 Mixing of chemicals by vehicular tracking must be avoided, unless it is done by design. (Later in the event it may become necessary to mix some of the spilled chemicals for neutralization or other reasons, but at that time the decision is based on a scientific rationale and is a planned event.)

Fig. 8-2 Use any tool available to stop the flow.

Garden tools and straw

There are few events in which first responders cannot pause for a few seconds and make a significant contribution with a shovel or a bale of straw (Figure 8-2). The boy with his finger in the dike comes to mind as more than a folk tale. Three or four shovelsful of dirt, tossed in a swale or indentation in the ground, have restrained the flow of a large volume of chemicals at wreck scenes many times. Fixed facilities always have existing (and usually obvious) drainage paths. A sack of sand or a few shovelsful of dirt can plug or impede flow. A keen eye for topographic relief and a quick observation of the directions in which the liquids are flowing should facilitate the placement of these flow restraints at critical points, and—it is hoped—before the spilled chemical reaches these points. Tools as crude as washtubs are often used to haul materials that may inhibit overland flow.

Dams and dikes

Frequently, it is necessary to use firefighting water* to flush and dilute a volatile liquid or to quench a fire. Water, for instance, may be used to transfer an imminent threat to a more remote location. However, the use of water generally increases the cost of cleanup exponentially. The principle here is that *the least water is the best water but not at the expense of safety.* When fire equipment arrives on-scene, there is reason to believe that some form of earth-moving equipment could also be brought in. A small tractor with a rear backhoe or a front bucket is as mobile as some fire units. Why shouldn't each fire department have such a piece of equipment? Forest rangers do have them and can thus respond to and isolate fires in minutes. Wouldn't it be practical to have a damming operation begin almost at the same time as application of water to the fire? The kinds of dikes and dams we are discussing are not things of beauty, nor are they products of any particular design. They are trial-and-error mounds of dirt placed by eyeball leveling and common sense, but if timely and effective, they may ultimately be worth millions of dollars. Such innovations may also prove extremely valuable to the scope of overall cleanup. Figure 8-3 shows how a small amount of earth, strategically placed, contained 500 gallons (1.9 m^3) of oil. Note how the interrupted flow around the "box culvert" has impounded the oil for easy recovery. Once the material is contained (keeping in mind the previously mentioned cautions), a number of things begin to happen.

1 The equilibration or normalization period is now foreseeable.

2 Time is available to plan for phase 2 and phase 3.

3 The pollution picture is much clearer.

4 Public safety, health, and welfare are enhanced.

* Hereafter, the water used for fighting fires will be called "fire water."

Fig. 8-3 A small dirt plug can trap a considerable amount of spilled material.

While water is being used, care must always be taken not to mix the chemicals that were successfully isolated and temporarily impounded by first responders.

Air Spills

Containment of air spills is so dangerous that it is not even addressed as a technique in this book. There is only a handful of experts in the United States who are competent to confront leaks of various volatile chemicals. To be sure, there are specialists in specific chemicals such as chlorine, ammonia, and liquid propane gas, but very few people can technically address the whole spectrum of pressurized gases and chemicals. There are, unfortunately, growing numbers of people who profess total competency but who are in fact extremely dangerous to the exercise. The person trained to put foam on a specific chemical cannot apply this knowledge as a complete technical package at a chemical warehouse fire. The person who can patch a chlorine car may have no experience with LPG. As an example of the complexity of air-spill containment, there are more than 60 different kinds of "patching" materials, with perhaps 1000 different application configurations, in current use. The applications range from welding to gluing. While they are leaking, many chemicals are subject to ignition or polymerization. The trigger for these events can be anything from water to sunlight. Sudden, unexpected ignition can be fatal either through fire and heat or through the effects of noxious or toxic gases. The process of polymerization (the combining of two or more small molecules to form larger molecules) often yields noxious gases that can be extremely dangerous to work with.

Frequently, the fire that we are so anxious to quench may be a blessing in disguise. The controlled burning of a chemical, even considering the noxious or toxic smoke, may be by far the *safest, quickest, least costly* method of mitigating the damage from that particular chemical.

The answer is a simple one—let the experts handle it. There are few if any hazardous substances accidents in which experts cannot be on-scene within 6 to 10 hours. The key is to obtain the correct experts and to feel certain that they are truly experts. Once again, the answer is simple—use the 1510 plan. The mobilization of response efforts in the United States is becoming a well-organized field. As an example, one phone call to the National Response Center (1-800-424-8802) can have scientific experts as well as trained chemical patching personnel on jet aircraft headed to the scene within 1 to 2 hours. This would certainly appear to be a strong endorsement of the waiting period between phase 1 and phase 2.

Water Spills

Perhaps 70 percent of all hazardous substance accidents are water-related. That is, natural streams and ponds are directly involved with the various chemicals. Containment is most difficult when large or moving bodies of water are receptors of the chemical.

It is important to remember that few chemicals or fuels can be diluted by hoses to the point that they are rendered harmless by that act alone. The classical error is to assume that gasoline washed from the interstate highway is gone. True, there is a mechanical emulsification which renders the immediate area generally safe from fire or explosion, but through swales, ditches, storm pipes, or overland flow the initial emulsion will reach a stream. The error does not lie in washing for safety, but in assuming that washing eliminates the entire problem. The same reasoning can apply even to soluble chemicals. There are simply not enough fire reserves to dilute many concentrated chemicals to the point that they are harmless. Even if 10 million gallons (38,000 m^3) of water were poured on a 10,000-gallon (38-m^3) spill of a technical grade organophosphate, it could still be present in lethal concentrations.

Once again, containment is paramount, certainly not in the median of the highway but at some point in the drainage system adjacent to the spill site. As with land spills, the earliest judgments will be significant factors in the scope of the overall problem. Basically, containment must be as near the source as possible. This of course limits to some degree the work area, the volume of water, and the affected area involved. Judgment, however, must be tempered with the consideration of other contingencies. For example, during the containment effort:

1 *Never* divert liquids to sanitary sewer lines. People have been killed at treatment plants by exploding gasoline; they have also been severely injured by volatile chemicals entering the plant.

2 *Never* trap volatile chemicals in closed conduits such as storm drains.

3 *Never* linger around impoundments of mixed chemicals.

4 *Never* allow smoking around the area.

Let's review some of the containment methods in use today. Figures 8-1 through 8-7 typify some of these methods, and Figures 8-8 through 8-14 illustrate them diagrammatically. Figure 8-8 depicts the use of the underflow dam mentioned earlier in the chapter. The advantages of the underflow system are quick assembly, trial-and-error improvisation, inexpensiveness, and utilization of materials which are available anywhere. The technical key is to avoid any vortex in the impoundment that could allow any floatable chemicals to pass downstream. Any mixing through turbulence of the light volatile fractions with the water will result in chemical or oil sheens appearing below the outfall. This is unavoidable, but even the light sheens can be extracted from the water's surface by many of the commercial sorbents available today. Figures 8-9 and 8-10 show some hasty methods using materials that can be found anywhere, transported by small truck or automobile, and hand carried on-scene. Figure 8-12 shows the application of commercial booms which are of course more effective. Figures 8-4 and 8-5 show two entirely different underflow dams in use. Figure 8-6 shows a homemade multipurpose dam that is really serving more as a boom than as a dam. Figure 8-7 illustrates how bridge piers can be used to contain booms fashioned from screen wire and a sorbent material. The idea here is that stream velocities prohibit the use of typical containment booms so we force the floatable liquid through a barrier of material that will absorb it. This barrier is called a sorbent boom. These

Fig. 8-4 Underflow dam made from a hollow log.

Fig. 8-5 A more sophisticated underflow dam.

Fig. 8-6 Homemade boom.

Fig. 8-7 Floating sorbent boom.

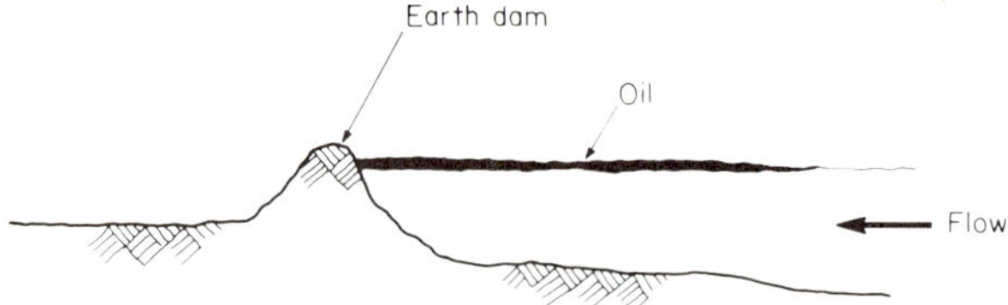

Fig. 8-8 A hastily constructed dam. Addition of a pipe will convert this into an underflow dam much like that in Figure 8-1.

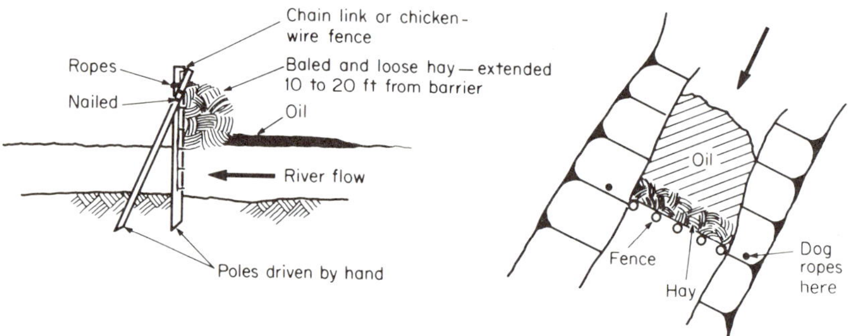

Fig. 8-9 A makeshift river barrier can be made from ordinary farm materials.

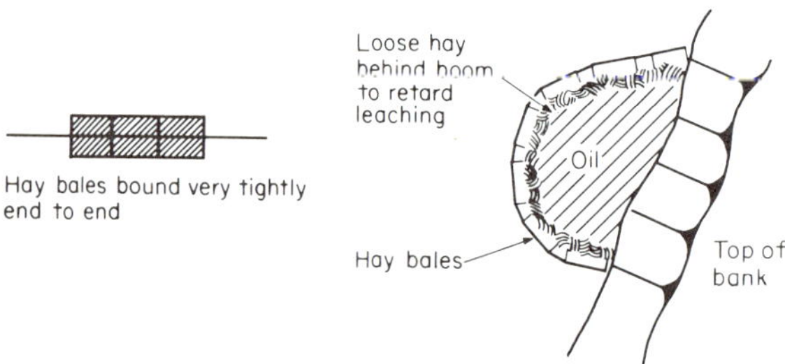

Fig. 8-10 Farm materials can also be used as a makeshift boom in a lake spill. This system is good for only 12 to 15 hours.

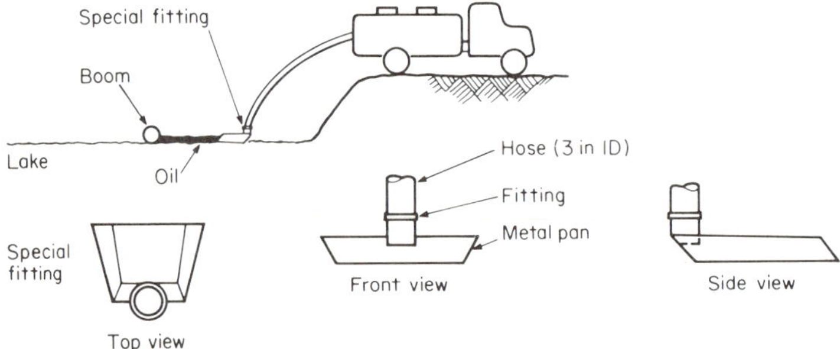

Fig. 8-11 A vacuum pump truck is used to remove contained oil. Tips: tighten boom as you remove oil; keep the oil thick. Devise a fitting for the end of the line; keep it handy. Use bottom draft trucks so you can bleed water off.

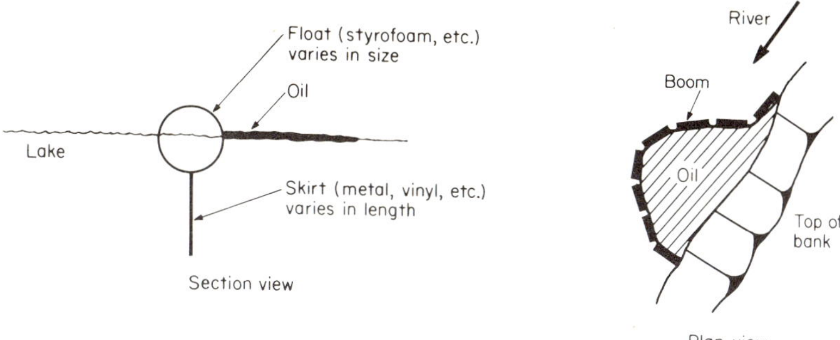

Fig. 8-12 A simple recovery technique using a commercial boom.

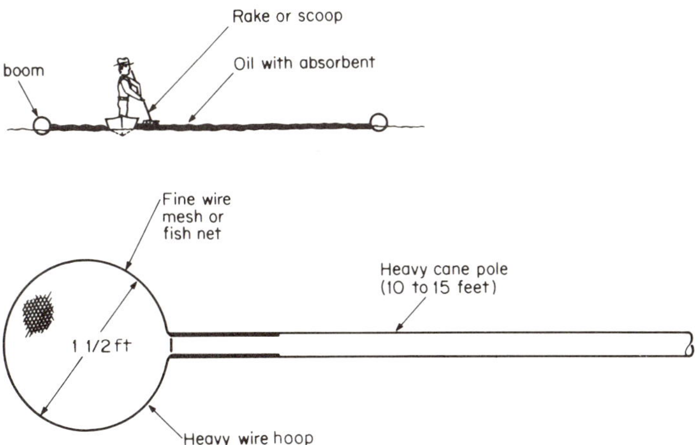

Fig. 8-13 Hand tools for recovery of absorbed materials.

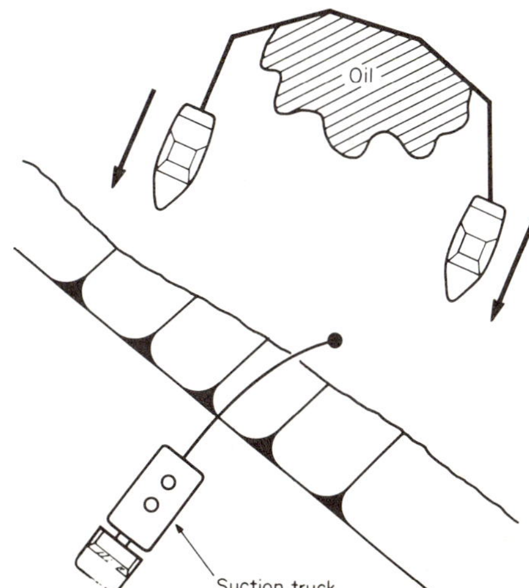

Fig. 8-14 Recovery of oil from lake surface.

are not perfect methods, but they are a means of doing something when doing nothing won't do. Their effectiveness is obviously variable.

8-2 RECOVERY

Recovery actually begins in phase 2 and extends into phase 3. It is highlighted by the philosophy that the chemical should be extracted from the soil or water in the most concentrated form that is practical and in the largest quantity possible. The amount of chemical recovered depends on factors such as:

1 Initial containment activities
2 The type of chemical
  (a) Health effects (toxicity, persistency)
  (b) Solubility, volatility
  (c) Viscosity (penetration characteristics)
3 Spill location, physical difficulties
4 Dilution
5 Time of soil or water exposure
6 Methods used
7 Weather

As with containment methods, every recovery method mentioned in this section has a scientific basis, even though its general appearance may lack ordinary good technical taste. Excluded from the text are curves and nomographs describing such things as flow through a closed pipe, pressure heads, dynamic friction heads, times to fill or empty cylindrical tanks, unit tables, drainage computations, or chemical volumetric relationships. Also missing are various chemical tables. The presumption is that these can be obtained from the technical references in Chapter 9 of this book. One of the references—*Manual for Control of Hazardous Materials Spills*—done for EPA in 1977 by Envirex (Milwaukee, Wisconsin) is excellent for those who wish to study the various sequences of spill-response technology. The document is available to the public through the National Technical Information Service, Springfield, VA 22161.

In this section we will be discussing expedient field methods that are tried and proven, no matter how simple their appearance. Once the material is contained to some reasonable extent, a scenario of recovery must be quickly developed. As the various components are selected, you must make as certain as possible that by selecting one component you have not totally precluded the use of other components. For example, the selection of sorbents to immobilize the floatable liquids may later limit the use of certain kinds of mechanical recovery equipment and at the same time increase the volume of disposables. Yet, sorbents may very well be required to limit soil penetration, or the spreading of chemicals on a large water surface, or as a containment method in certain spills. Let's examine some of the land- and water-oriented recovery methods that are frequently used today.

Fig. 8-15 Access road of crushed limestone.

Land

The mixing of chemicals with soil is always a problem. No spill scene can reasonably be left if the soil is significantly contaminated. A better understanding of this principle can be gained by reviewing the EPA's regulations implementing the Resource Conservation and Recovery Act. Assuming that we know what residual level of chemicals we can leave in the soil, we can examine various methods of recovery. Of course we need access to the area. Figure 8-15 shows an access road being constructed. Note that it is being built of crushed limestone, an excellent buffer for acid compounds. With caution, such a road may also serve as a dike or dam.

The extent of soil contamination must be determined. To this end, soil testing in a necessity. Mobile labs are available to the RRT and certainly make this chore less difficult. Beyond soil testing, it may be necessary to search for buried debris or, as in Figure 8-16, buried drums of chemicals.

Fig. 8-16 Special army teams use metal detectors to search for buried drums of chemicals.

Fig. 8-17 Sorbent materials stockpiled near a chemical spill.

If the chemical is contained in pools on the land surface, specially treated, commercially available sorbents are useful. These sheets, beads, or shredded fabric-like particles may be placed directly in the oil, gasoline, or various other chemicals, and by acting like giant blotters, sorb the liquid. Figure 8-17 shows three different sorbents used in a 1979 chemical spill in the Midwest. Some of these products sorb up to 40 times their weight in liquid, so keep in mind the recovery problem in using a heavy roll of this material. Although largely unproven in the field at this writing, laboratory tests suggest that some sorbents, as well as activated carbon, may even draw or sorb liquids from soil bodies—an interesting possibility.

When a chemical has penetrated the ground and we have a reasonable knowledge of the area and depth affected, there are several recovery techniques available.

Trenching

Trenching is a common method of leaching materials from natural soil bodies. The idea is to interrupt subsurface gradients and take advantage of

Fig. 8-18 Leaching trenches at a spill site.

the soil's porosity. Care must be taken not to break through underlying impervious layers or to penetrate "perched" water tables. Trial core borings will be helpful here. Figure 8-18 shows a typical trenching operation.

Usually a herringbone configuration provides maximum leaching. Many situations involving floatable chemicals are greatly benefited by the careful use of water injection. Remember, however, that after this use, the water must be considered a pollutant until shown to be otherwise. Also, some states prohibit such water injection altogether. If it is believed that water injection is a realistic solution entrust the operation to someone experienced in that technique. The RRT should help in these kinds of technical decisions.

Pumping

Well-point pumping systems are becoming more frequently used as a mechanism for removing chemicals from soil bodies. Chemicals that are soluble or partially soluble present the subsurface characteristics of ground water. In homogeneous soils, many chemicals penetrate and form a concentration bulb. The theory is that if you can empty this bulb by pumping all liquids from it, you should get both water and the contaminant. Experience has shown that where this system works at all it usually works well. Consequently, the possibility of success can usually be determined early and with minimal pilot studies. Figure 8-19 is an example of a highly successful well-point operation following a 1978 train derailment.

Excavation

Technically, excavation is at the "bottom of the barrel," although it is still used frequently even today. There are times that excavation must be used as a recovery method, but modern landfill rules and regulations prompted by RCRA now make this choice very costly. In reality this method only transfers

Fig. 8-19 A well-point pumping operation.

the problem, as in most cases the material dug up is simply buried somewhere else. The technologies of incineration, solvent extraction, neutralization by mixing, or biological degradation are bright hopes but are largely undeveloped. Moreover, some states have laws prohibiting some of these activities. The bulk of the material defeats incineration capabilities available today, and neutralization is scrutinized carefully by RCRA regulations. Consequently, as of today, these new concepts are still not practical as component tools for the functional cleanup package.

The cost of taking excavated material to "secured" land fills is astronomical. In 1981 costs for disposal alone ran from $14 to $80 per drum, depending on the chemical. Cost of transportation ranges from $4 to $20 per drum, and a DOT-approved drum costs around $25. Add to all of this the tests required to identify what is in the drum, and you have some idea of the problem.

On the drawing board

Concepts currently in various stages of development are giving us reason to believe that help is on the way:

1 *Microwaves* The idea that microwaves can be directed at and destroy some chemicals in soil is being given some research consideration.

2 *Direct heat* The concept of directing intense heat at thin layers of contaminated soil is being looked at.

EPA is doing some exciting research on these two concepts and others at their research laboratory in Edison, New Jersey. Some very sophisticated research in computerized systems is being done jointly by the EPA research lab in Cincinnati, Ohio, and the Corps of Engineers waterways experiment station at Vicksburg, Mississippi. These projects cannot bear fruit soon enough.

Water

Surface

Floatable substances contained on the surface of water bodies are recoverable in varying degrees. Our capability in this area grows daily, with oil-spill technology leading the way. Although there is a massive arsenal of equipment available today, many of the simplest techniques are still valuable to us. Figures 8-12 through 8-14 again illustrate some of the simplest of these. There are commercial skimming devices of every size, shape, and functional mode that you can think of. The cost in 1981 of one skimmer ranges from $200 to $20,000. Booms of every shape and material are available. The cost of booms in 1981 runs from $6 to $50 per foot for inland equipment. Sorbents for virtually anything are commercially available. Vacuum trucks designed specifically for spill recovery are becoming abundant. Figure 8-20 shows two of these modern machines at a 1979 oil spill.

Fig. 8-20 Modern vacuum/pump trucks in use.

The beauty of Figure 8-20 is that the equipment is real, available, and can be found all over the United States and in other countries as well. There is a vast quantity of literature available that shows the various applications of the recovery equipment on the market. The reader can obtain these materials with little effort. Look in the Yellow Pages under "Oil Spill Recovery," or call the nearest U.S. Coast Guard or EPA office.

The success of recovery largely depends on the effectiveness of containment. Some strategies used in containment so enhance recovery that large-volume pickup can be accomplished by simply parking a vacuum truck at the edge of the stream and pumping directly from the oil pool.

The cost of renting these vacuum trucks ranges (in 1981) from $35 to $75 per hour, depending on the size and capability of the truck. Septic tank service trucks are also extremely valuable in this kind of operation.

Figure 8-21 shows the correct deployment of a boom in a river. The floating material will collect in the angle formed by the boom with the shore of the stream. A secondary floating or sorbent boom will usually be required to skim the material that ducks the primary boom. Be sure to dig the skirt of the boom

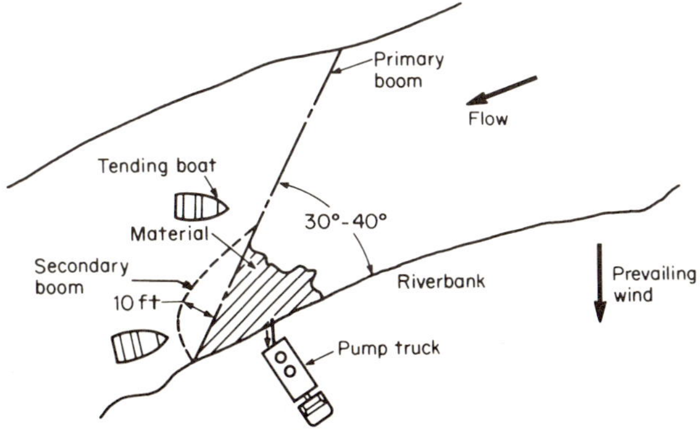

Fig. 8-21 Boom deployment in a river.

in at the point where it merges with the shore. *Always* keep tending boats down stream and away from the boom, since most booms can be submerged with little effort. Figure 8-22 shows a method referred to as *scupping*. Its principle is use of the prevailing wind and slower bank velocities to force the floating material into a series of small shoreline pits. This method should facilitate pumping. As a side note, where floating, oillike materials are involved, a 10- to 15-knot wind will dominate river currents up to 2 feet per second (0.61 m/s). The wind is always a *very* significant factor. Don't ignore it—use it. There are other gimmicks that can be used, such as taking advantage of wind and natural eddies where the material will eddy out (actually pool at the shoreline) on its own.

Surface containment on a stream or lake is shaky at best. The logistical problems encountered in getting trucks to the entrapped material usually involve wasted time, loss of material, and extra costs. If land is available, it is always best to pump the material directly into a pit as shown in Figure 8-23. The size of this pit can vary but should allow for continual pumping from the stream to minimize the residence time of the material in the water, where it is subject to all sorts of contingencies. Later, too, trucks can pump a purer form of the material from the pit because there has been time for separation. While access to booms can be limited, the material in pits is always accessible to the trucks, and no standby time is required.

There are times that stream bypass or diversion can be useful, especially if velocities are a problem. The trick here is to take the stream flow from the channel through a diversion ditch equipped with containment devices. To slow down the stream, make the diversion gradient very flat. Of course there will be a larger gradient fall at the lower end, but the entire system is only temporary and can be managed for a short time. Figure 8-24 diagrams such an operation. Be careful of state laws and riparian rights when using this technique. They are a problem for the RRT. When these operations are

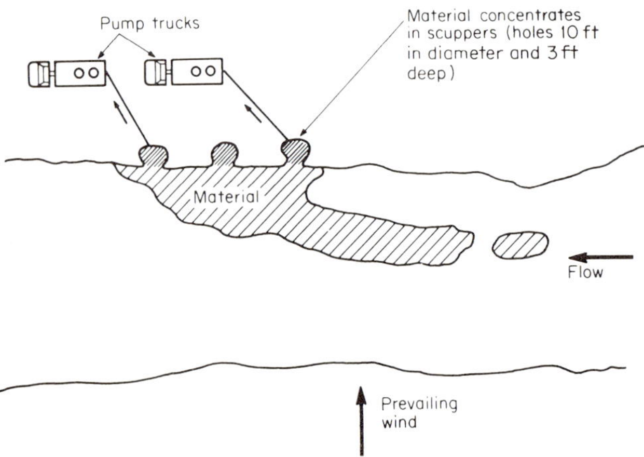

Fig. 8-22 Man-made pits (scuppers) in river bank that aid in recovery.

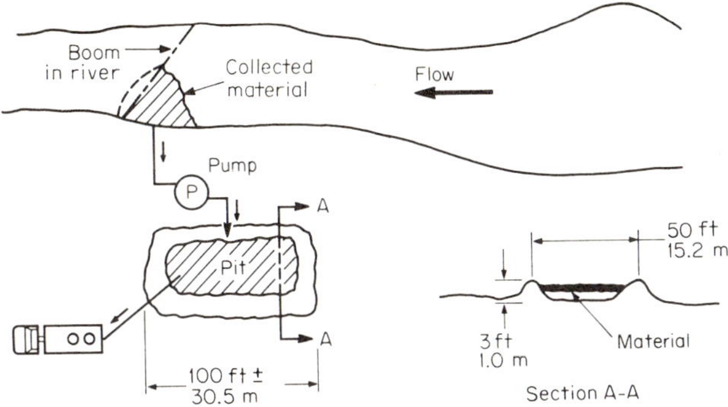

Fig. 8-23 Off-stream storage.

over, the site must be restored. Backfills and surface scars must be graded and seeded, and debris must be removed. Be prepared to pay reasonable damages to the property owners. Ninety percent of the time the owner of the damaged property is cooperative if treated fairly.

Solubles and emulsions

Where the chemical is soluble or has been emulsified, recovery is really difficult but, in many cases, not impossible. Organics that are subject to activated-carbon adsorption and chemicals that will precipitate out with pH change are good examples of such chemicals. Usually a simple tabletop experiment will determine whether a recovery method is practical. If so, the hardware devices for field use are reasonably simple.

Using Activated Carbon or Peat Moss Various entrapment devices that allow containment of the carbon or moss but passage of the stream flow are easily constructed of window-screen wire, plastic pipes, plywood, and rough lumber. Take a closer look at Figure 8-7. A box of plywood and screen wire could just as easily have been placed across each span. It takes little imagination to develop a system that will suit the need. Dams of peat moss (where carbon is unavailable) will frequently recover a respectable quantity of dissolved organics. Activated carbon adsorption of many chemicals is often greatly enhanced by a pH adjustment prior to carbon filtration. If carefully constructed and maintained (changing the carbon or moss periodically), such devices have been known to remove 90 to 98 percent of organic chemicals in the 10 to 100 mg/L range. Higher concentrations are a real problem and require larger carbon exposure.

Precipitation Often it is practical to force a chemical from solution, or from what appears to be a solution. One of the methods most frequently used involves inducing a sudden, dramatic pH change in the whole liquid mass. The precipitating material will floc and either float or sink. The settling of the floc can often be hastened by the addition of small amounts of alum. The material can then be recovered with conventional tools designed for mud pumping from the bottom or skimming from the surface.

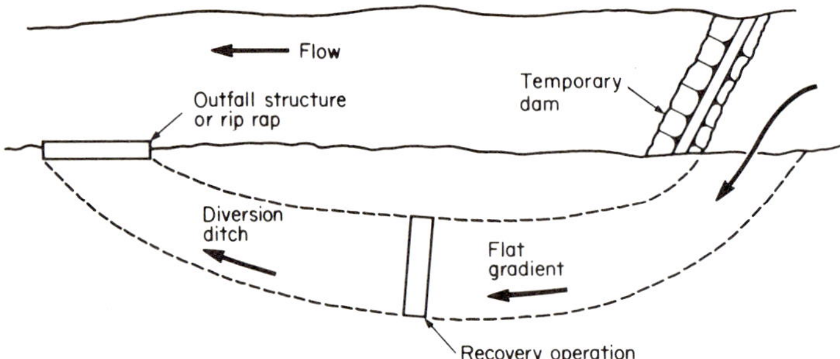

Fig. 8-24 Stream bypass or diversion ditch.

While there have been many successes using the two concepts above, they are both more effective under controlled conditions such as obtain in the diversion-ditch method shown in Figure 8-24, or in slow-moving, well-defined streams.

8-3 TREATMENT SYSTEMS

When the material that has caused all the concern is contained, recovered, and placed in secure locations such as reservoirs, sumps, or containers, what is the next step? One of the first thoughts that comes to mind is reuse or recycling. Chemicals and fuels are expensive. Without mentioning the price of gasoline or fuel oil, consider that one tank car of a specific pesticide may be valued at $500,000 (1981). Despite all the quick action required on-scene, a concerted effort should always be made to recover the spilled chemical in the purest form and the largest amount possible. As a practical matter, this has not typified the hazardous substance accident scene in the past. Where chemicals are concerned, recovery technology has been lacking. Oil and gasoline spills, however, are a different story. At one spill in Alabama in the early 1970s, 75 percent of a million-gallon (3800-m^3) spill of #2 fuel oil was recovered from a river, placed in tank trucks, and transported to settling tanks at a terminal facility. In a few weeks it was placed directly back in the pipeline from which it had spilled, transported up the East Coast, and delivered to the consumer. It was as simple as that. There is reason to believe that as we become more competent in chemical-spill technology and research, more techniques and hardware will reach the field. When this occurs, recovery for recycling should become a realistic and routine part of the chemical cleanup scenario. Beyond recovery there still remain liquid residuals or areas of contaminated soils that must be treated to some extent. This phase of the cleanup operation is the most unpredictable in terms of costs and time.

Treatment Parameters

How clean is clean? This is undoubtedly the most difficult question to be answered during phases 2 and 3. When deciding how much contaminant can safely be left in the environment, many things must be considered:

1 Existing legal limits for materials in the environment (RCRA, state and local laws, water quality limits)
2 Private property and riparian water rights
3 Nature of the contaminant, especially its persistence in the environment
4 Costs
5 Safety and public health
6 Limitations, e.g. physical impossibility
7 Testing
8 Quarantine
9 Residual disposal

Once again there is a clear mandate for committee-type decisions that can only be accomplished by an organization such as the RRT. The various goals must be established here, and only by responsible persons who have the authority and backing of their agencies. These kinds of decisions control the effectiveness and overall cost of cleanup and should not be subjected to bureaucratic afterthought, paper shuffling, or quasi-decisions mixed with reputation-saving alternatives. What is required here, in addition to quick, crisp, timely decisions, is a set of cleanup parameters based on the above nine considerations and applied to the specific situation. To vary a cleanup criterion even slightly once the operation is underway may very well add significantly to the overall cost.

Treatment of Liquids

Once a decision on the cleanup limits is made, it is reasonable to conduct simple tests to determine which, if any, system will work to achieve these limits. The idea, of course, will be to concentrate and extract the contaminant so that the bulk of liquid remaining will be water clean enough to be returned to the lake, stream, river, or sanitary sewerage system.

Treatment possibilities are numerous, including:

- Carbon adsorption
- pH adjustment
- Air stripping and aeration
- Precipitation

- Neutralization
- Biological (conventional systems)
- Destruction
- Dilution
- Mixing
- Land spraying

The above items, singly or in combination, may prove very useful because they are simple and expedient. Table 8-1 is a chart listing some of the more frequently spilled chemicals. It is designed to give the reader some initial directions in setting up small-scale testing. (*By no means* is this chart intended for anything more.) There are many times however, when necessity requires you to act before the experts arrive. Experience has shown that a hasty analysis of the spilled product (using Table 8-1) should put your initial reactions reasonably in line with the techniques that will be used in phase 3. The point here is to minimize lost time, money, and effort, as well as to avoid dangers by having at least a basic direction in which to proceed. It is obvious that a chart such as this could be greatly expanded.

Carbon adsorption

Activated carbon is a frequently used treatment device in cleaning up after hazardous substance accidents. Certainly it is not perfect, having a number of limitations such as:

1 Grain size (equipment problems)
2 Cost
3 Availability
4 Disposal and/or regeneration

It is important to note that the use of carbon, even if later proved technically valueless, really adds no danger to the situation. Moreover, as reflected in Table 8-2, some rather dramatically successful results have been achieved in the field, even with very crude techniques. Can you think of a better trial and error approach when time is critical and some kind of action must be taken? Also, consider the facts that field testing is quick, cheap, and reasonably accurate, and the treatment system can be quite simple in concept and construction. This is why carbon treatment is a favorite. During the year 1978–1979, however, the price of activated carbon skyrocketed. In the future, cost increases could very well limit its broad use unless developments such as the carbon regenerator shown in Figure 8-33 (page 123) are put to use. This unit, tested by EPA at its Edison, New Jersey, laboratory, came into use in mid-1980.

Carbon treatment methods can range from flash mixing the carbon in drums and settling it out in open pits to very sophisticated mechanical devices. Figures 8-25 through 8-27 show how used garbage dumpsters were placed

Table 8-1. Treatment Systems to Be Pilot Tested in Chemical Spills

	Pilot tests to be considered									
Spilled chemical	Carbon adsorption	pH adjustment	Air stripping	Precipitation	Neutralization	Biological	Destruction	Dilution	Mixing	Land spraying
Chlorinated hydrocarbon	1					2				
Organophosphate	2	1				4				3
Chlorine					1			3	2	4
Acid					1			3	2	4
Caustic					1			3	2	4
Ammonia		1	2					3		4
White phosphorus							1			
Isobutyronitrile	3	2	1							
Acrylonitrile	3	2	1							
Volatile organic substances	3	2	1							4
Latex				1						

NOTE: These are possible steps, in numerical order. Certain chemicals or mixtures and the surrounding contingencies may suggest more or fewer steps.

Table 8-2. Activated-Carbon Treatment Results—Actual Spill Conditions

	Analyses of treatment system samples					
	Influent			Effluent		
Date	PCB, ppb	COD, mg/L	Carbon, ppm	PCB, ppb	COD, mg/L	% Removal of PCB's
9/20/76	. . .	369	27.0	<0.2	66	
9/25/76	0.73	. . .	10.7	ND	399	
9/26/76	0.56	1068	10.7	ND	282	
9/28/76	2.22	. . .	10.2	0.26	. . .	88
9/29/76	7.7	988	10.2	0.4	419	94
9/30/76	0.93	932	28.6	0.99	394	
10/1/76	1.49	942	28.6	0.29	463	80
10/6/76	1.15	1068	25.9	0.14	399	87
10/7/76	0.66	1000	43.5	<0.2	571	70
10/8/76	0.62	1225	43.5	<0.2	372	61

SOURCE: 1975 study by the author and others of an improvised treatment system installed at Whitehouse, Florida. Unpublished technical report by Region IV EPA, Atlanta, Georgia.

Fig. 8-25 Dumpsters lined up to form a treatment system.

together, sealed against leakage, equipped with an aerator for air stripping, and loaded with limestone for pH adjustment and activated carbon for organic adsorption; the setup actually was 98 percent effective in treating organic solvents and water. Figures 8-28 through 8-32, together with Table

Fig. 8-26 pH adjustment.

Fig. 8-27 Activated-carbon system at work.

Fig. 8-28 Homemade flash mixer.

Fig. 8-29 Settling basin.

Fig. 8-30 Equipment housing.

8-2 and Figure 8-35, depict a similar system (excluding aeration) constructed by utilizing partially developed terrain features, an old shed, some drums, plastic pipe, and a makeshift batching system. Remember, be positive and, at the same time, be flexible; do not anguish over pipe sizes, pump capacities, or carbon dosage. Test the effluent and make adjustments as needed. Notice in Figures 8-27 to 8-32 the general appearance of the treatment in progress. Millions of gallons of PCB-affected water and sludges were treated at a cost of $200,000 (1975 dollars). The final result is shown in Figure 8-32. Most

Fig. 8-31 An activated-carbon treatment system in construction (see Figure 8-38).

Fig. 8-32 The cleanup area complete with impervious surface crown.

chlorinated hydrocarbons are vulnerable to carbon adsorption, but a pH rise prior to carbon mixing generally enhances the efficiency of the operation.

Government and industry between them command several mobile carbon treatment units. Figures 8-36 through 8-38 show one of Calgon's units, O.H. Materials' skid unit, and EPA's emergency response unit, respectively. Information on cost, capacity, and various uses of these devices can be obtained by writing the Calgon Corporation, Box 1346, Pittsburgh, PA 15230; USEPA

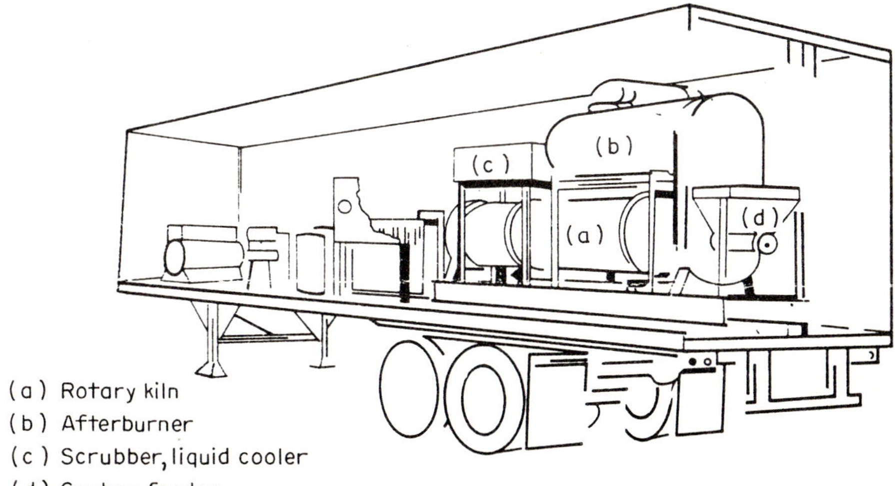

Fig. 8-33 Activated-carbon regenerator. (See discussion on page 120.)

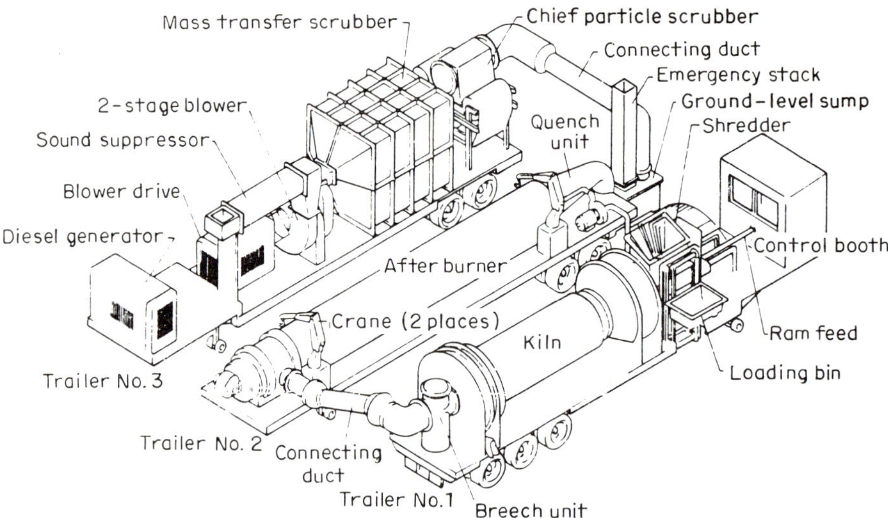

Fig. 8-34 Mobile incinerator (trailers are normally in line). (See discussion on page 130.)

Industrial Environmental Research Laboratory, Edison, NJ 08817; or O.H. Materials, Findlay, OH 45840.

pH adjustment

A sharp rise in pH has proven most successful in treating the organophosphate family, while in such cases as those involving ammonia, lowering the

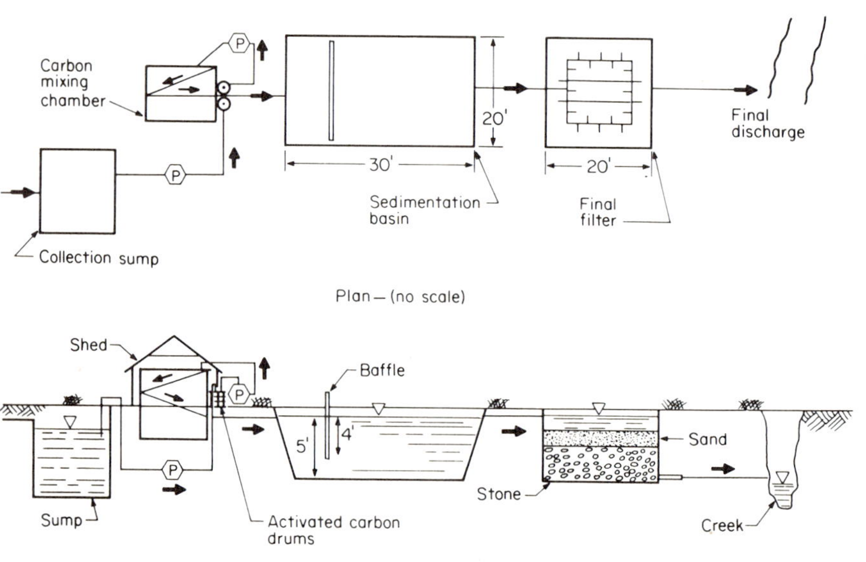

Fig. 8-35 An activated-carbon treatment system for use in the field.

Fig. 8-36 Calgon's mobile carbon treatment system.

Fig. 8-37 OH Materials' skid unit in operation.

pH is the operative method. When it is obvious that the same end result is achieved whether you raise or lower pH, consider going basic (raising pH). Alkaline materials are generally more available locally than acids. The treatment hardware in implementing a pH adjustment is very simple. A pit in which an acid solution, a caustic compound, or a basic medium (crushed lime) can be mixed with the contaminated liquid is usually adequate. A typical hasty

Fig. 8-38 An EPA emergency response unit.

Fig. 8-39 A chemical mixing pit.

mix pit is shown in Figure 8-39. The most important factor in this type of operation is mixing. Either a flow-through device to force contact (such as shown in Figure 8-35) or a mechanical mixing device will usually be necessary to achieve good results. Generally with this kind of treatment the goal is to change a chemical into a less toxic form so that the liquids can be discharged into a stream or sewer line. Once again, effluent testing will be the means of deciding when and where to discharge the final effluent.

Air stripping and aeration

These two concepts are particularly valuable in treating the various industrial solvents. Either process or both can also be used as a valuable component in a larger, more complicated system. Air stripping involves spraying the con-

Fig. 8-40 Air stripping.

Fig. 8-41 Land spraying.

taminated liquid into the air. Molecular separation allows the volatilization of the unstable fractions. Figure 8-40 shows a simple pumping operation used to spray water contaminated with acrylonitrile into the air. The final effluent is allowed to fall in a thin sheet over the soil, and if the treatment is effective, there should be no persistent stream or soil contamination. If necessary, collect the runoff and repeat stripping. Figure 8-41 is a good example of air stripping as a component of land spraying, a technique to be discussed briefly in this section. Fire hoses, lawn sprinklers, and a simple water pump may be used to accomplish air stripping.

Aeration is a related but different technique. Here oxygen or air is bubbled through the contaminated liquid as shown in Figure 8-42. The result is forced

Fig. 8-42 In-stream aeration in progress.

volatilization of the light fractions and oxygen saturation of the liquid mass. Compressed air and/or oxygen under pressure can usually be piped into the liquid body. Any time that air stripping or aeration is used, all persons in close proximity to the operation should be made to wear *at least* some form of breathing apparatus.

Precipitation

Materials that present themselves in colloidal suspension rather than in solutions may be precipitated out, settled, and recovered. Latex is a good example. A sharp pH change will serve as a precipitating agent and will also cause the particles to collect and flocculate. An addition of 5 to 10 mg/L of alum will cause the floc to float in one mass. Once this occurs, conventional skimming techniques can be used to recover the latex material. If the precipitated material is too thick or bulky to skim, remove it from the surface with shovels and rakes. Precipitation of suspended chemicals generally poses interesting possibilities. This is an area that deserves more research.

Neutralization

The word neutralization as used here refers to pH deviations caused by acidity or alkalinity. Many bodies of liquids incident to a spill situation are pollutants simply because they are on the acid or basic side of neutral pH. The neutralization, then, of such a contaminated liquid is a practical remedy. A warning is issued here not to confuse simple acidity or alkalinity with a toxic pH deviation. Do not assume, for example, that a pH below or above 7.0 is simply a pH problem. Many toxicants cause a pH change the adjustment of which does nothing to mitigate the toxic dangers. If, however, there is only a pH problem, the adjustment is a matter of mixing in acid or alkaline material

Fig. 8-43 Mixing lime with 98% concentrated sulfuric acid.

and sampling after a reasonable length of time. Do not dump in a pound of hydrated lime for each pound of acid spilled. Insert a length of litmus paper, be disappointed, and then dump in more lime. Remember the mixing and equilibration time. Conduct some tabletop tests to determine the mix ratio and time needed for proper neutralization. Your goal is to reach a reasonable pH (6.5 to 7.5) without creating a massive sediment problem by adding too much acid or base in haste. A handy means of mixing lime into the acid is the driving force of fire hoses. It is quite practical to get close enough to the pit to direct the hoses with force into the lime and acid, thus mixing the two chemicals. Take a closer look at Figure 8-43. As a basic compound is mixed with a concentrated acid, tremendous local vapor clouds are caused by the heat energy released. These clouds can be noxious for several hundred feet but are generally not considered fatal. A simple organic breathing mask is usually adequate protection against this particular vapor. Involvement with such vapors for extended lengths of time, however, is not recommended.

Biological

Biological treatment is a definite possibility if it is practical from a logistics standpoint and environmentally acceptable. Many contaminated liquids can be treated to the point that they can be hauled, piped, or pumped to a conventional sewage treatment plant for final biological treatment.

For example, it is often possible to use one or a combination of these hasty treatment schemes on-scene in order to reduce the concentration of contaminant to the point that a conventional treatment plant can receive and treat the bulk liquid without a disruption of its general treatment operation. This should not be attempted unless a brief but thorough treatability study has been done. The correct blend can be determined and the release flow can be controlled to accomodate it. In this case, the biological treatment is not the system used on-scene, it is the treatment given at the sewage treatment plant.

In the future it will sometimes be practical to construct modular biological treatment systems on-scene when the liquid bulk is large enough or there is perhaps a continual flow of contaminant that will leach and pollute for a long period of time. These systems are still largely experimental.

Destruction

Never a popular decision but at times a necessary one is the destruction of certain products. Destruction is the on-site or remote burning or detonation of the contaminant. White phosphorus is an example. When explosive techniques are required, don't try it on your own; call 1-800-424-8802. Ask for the phone number of the appropriate EPA regional spill person, who will activate the Army Explosive Ordinance Demolition team (EOD). Everyone can work together on this one. Remember the RRT?

Burning is a related method and can be used tactically in dangerous situations. The assumption is, of course, that enough knowledge has been gained through observation to reasonably predict the type and extent of the burn. Also, the area must be properly evacuated and absolutely secure. This again is a decision for the RRT, which must weigh the arguments for and against.

Burning of residuals, concentrated sludges, and debris may have become a reality by 1981. Through its research laboratory in Cincinnati, Ohio, EPA is developing a mobile incinerator which is without doubt the dream of those in the spill business. Figure 8-34 (page 124) is a rendition of the device, the capabilities of which are fantastic. There will be more data available on this system later, but for now it is basically designed to be mobile; to operate at high temperatures; to destroy almost any chemical whether involved with soil, sludges, or liquids; and to grind and destroy debris as big as railroad ties.

Dilution

For various reasons and under specific circumstances, it may be necessary to dilute the contaminant to environmentally acceptable limits and release it. This method should always be at the bottom of the list of alternatives and viewed as only slightly better than leaving the problem there. This method is simply asking the environment to assimilate something foreign to it. If this must be done, then make it a team decision and carefully calculate the blend prior to release. There should be state water quality officials available to provide guidance on water quality standards and desired release parameters. Again, the RRT should make this decision.

Mixing

By building simple batching and mixing ponds and allowing the various products to blend, spilled chemicals can frequently be combined to form a much less toxic liquid. Ammonia and acid, as well as chlorine and caustic are examples. Usually the combined liquid can be neutralized as to pH, and the sediments, salts of acids, etc., treated as solid hazardous wastes and removed. This method is entirely different from that discussed under *Neutralization* above. There we were discussing the neutralization of a single contaminant; here we are considering mixing several contaminants. There are big differences in the logistic and scientific considerations. When an attempt is made to mix several spilled chemicals, nothing is added to the problem in terms of materials and chemicals, but the physical operation is tricky and demands caution. The physical techniques are usually crude and the reactions more violent than the controlled releases described under neutralization. Several surge ponds can be constructed, or the quantities that are contained in the various dikes and dams can be brought together by ditching, piping, or pumping. The flows, however, must be controllable. Batter boards with V-notch weirs may be used, for example, but any method must allow for an all-out release and total mix when necessary.

Land spraying

One of the newer concepts in spill cleanup is the controversial method of land spraying or land treatment. Here the contaminated liquid is sprayed over a large land area and exposed to whatever treatment nature will give it. This is not always a popular idea, but it is being given very serious scientific considerations today as a realistic biological treatment scheme for sewage and some chemicals. The scientific considerations are complicated, and no such operation should be undertaken without a thorough treatability study. Factors such as vapors, penetration, bacterial decomposition, precipitation, runoff, security, land use, and safety must be carefully considered. Once again, this solution (if it proves to be one) would logically apply to the long-term operation in which treatment may last a year or more. Figure 8-41 shows a simply constructed system at work. Long-term site testing will always be necessary.

8-4 *IN SITU* TREATMENT

None of the methods described in Section 8-3, can be termed *in-place (in situ) treatment* in the strict sense. This particular concept involves treating the pollutant right where it is found. Many people view *in situ* amelioration as a "sweep it under the carpet" or "let nature do it" kind of solution. Not so—not if it is a carefully conceived, executed, and monitored operation. It is quite true, however, that much research must be done before this operation can be considered a routine cleanup system for certain accidents.

Bacterial Seeding

Some states permit the injection or spreading of bacterial cultures over certain soils or liquids contaminated by pollutants. The theory is that certain bacteria, whether aerobic (living in oxygen) or anaerobic (living totally free of oxygen), will actually feed on the contaminant. Acclimation of these particular bacteria to the contaminant, i.e., development of one suited to engage and consume the particular contaminant will actually expedite the degradation of the contamination. This is achieved when the contaminant is reduced to the metabolic by-products of the particular bacterium used—a natural process as old as time. The new trick is to force acceleration of the degradation process by the use of the appropriately grown bacteria. The acclimation, of course, results in the acceleration of the entire cleanup process. This final result will amount to a savings in time (months to years) over that required by natural degradation and, of course, will cause minimum site disturbance. Such a solution has been attempted several times in this country with varying degrees of success. In the early 1970s, EPA and others conducted research on this concept in oil spill cleanups. The concern that was expressed then, and one that is still around today, is bacteria control. How do we ensure without any doubt that we are cultivating harmless bacteria. In an effort to grow a hearty, virile, hungry bacterium, some tests have indicated that we may be providing conditions for the growth of pathogenic bacteria such as the *Salmonella* group. This possibility, however, is not enough reason to abandon the idea. First, there is no conclusive evidence that the growth of pathogenic organisms is a typical event or that this growth cannot be ultimately controlled; second, Mother Nature may allow the growth to proceed. In light of what we see ahead in RCRA (Section 8-5), think of the possibilities such a concept offers for both massive spill sites and abandoned waste sites.

Before ever attempting such an operation in the field, the following factors must be carefully evaluated:

1 Drainage and precipitation (physical migration)
2 Localization, i.e., barriers to contain the biological process
3 Laws that may be operative in the area
4 Continual testing
5 Land and water use

Physical, Chemical, and Biological Quarantine

If left in the environment, most contaminants are eventually neutralized in terms of harmfulness. Natural processes, such as hydrolysis, dilution, biodegradation, oxidation, and pH variation, are always available to attack essentially anything that insults a natural environment. The problem, as mentioned earlier, is time. Once again, it may be concluded from an overall assessment of the situation that if the area can be secured, i.e., localized in contamination effect as well as protected from use for a predetermined period of time, quarantine may be appropriate. Quarantine of a land area will amount to:

1 A declaration by the state or local health officials
2 Erection of security fencing
3 Placement of warning placards
4 Building of subsurface barriers and/or continual testing for migration
5 Consideration of drainage factors

The quarantine of a water body may amount to closing water supplies until the chemical passes. Ultimately nature will either dilute or degrade the contaminant. Any way you rationalize it, quarantine is a nice word for "letting nature do it" and therefore should not be employed except in rare circumstances.

Fixation

There are chemicals that can be *fixed* by being mixed or blended with commercially available soil preparations. Certain chemical and physical bonding will take place that will prevent migration. There are also products available that act as sealants, preventing migration by forming a gel on the bottom of ponds and pits. There are also viscous materials that can be injected into the ground around a contaminated area, thus creating an impervious barrier. Technology in this field is fairly advanced. Literature outlining many of these applications can be obtained by writing to such firms as the American Colloid Company in Skokie, Illinois.

Drainage and Precipitation Protection

Surface drainage is a must. The basic goal here is to cut off and redirect surface runoff, keeping it from the area affected by the accident. Usually this can be quickly achieved by means of shallow drain swales cut around the area with such equipment as a motor patrol or small crawler tractor. Windrowed dikes can supplement these. After as much cleanup and disposal as is practical, it may be desirable to place an impervious *crown* over the treated area to prevent precipitation penetration. Figure 8-32 is a good example of a fixation operation, complete with a clay turtle-back crown.

8-5 DISPOSAL

Final disposal of residual hazardous substances is a very difficult problem associated with the accident. No matter what form the Resource Conservation and Recovery Act (RCRA) finally takes in terms of regulations and enforcement, disposal of hazardous wastes is going to be expensive and time-consuming. The days of taking just anything to a landfill for burial are over. America, aroused by the sudden realization in the late 1970s that dangerous chemical wastes have been buried or stored all over the country, is up in arms. Landfills are one of the hottest political potatoes around anywhere, and the issues relate not to trash and garbage but to the landfill's potential for receiving hazardous waste materials. Secure landfills, considered as technically safe as money and modern technology can make them, have been enjoined from operation by the courts in several states. Incinerators designed to destroy almost any toxic liquid and as safely as is technically possible have also been enjoined. In a large Southern metropolitan area, the chairman of the county commission and a superior court judge, forced by circumstances to locate a large landfill in their community, were both soundly beaten at the polls. Location of the landfill was without question the key issue. The residual soil and chemical mixture from a 1974 train derailment is still loaded on six gondola cars on a rail siding in a Southwestern state. The mix is harmless, but no one has the money to dispose of it because the waste has the stigma of being hazardous. To take it to one of the four secure landfills in the surrounding 10 states would be ridiculously expensive. Federal, state, and local waste regulators are under tremendous pressure to establish safe hazardous landfills. If you think Three Mile Island was a hot issue, try buying a tract of land and starting up a hazardous waste landfill.

The Resource Conservation and Recovery Act (RCRA) envisions that by the early 1980s there will be an adequate number of secure hazardous landfills over the United States to practically and safely bury hazardous wastes that have been reduced to the smallest volume possible. Government regulators, however, are experiencing tough public reaction to any kind of landfill. In the meantime, government officials are also under pressure when using RCRA regulations for disposal of anything that is found by various formulas to be hazardous. What this means is best illustrated by the following, somewhat oversimplified example. Let's say a truck carrying waste oil overturns and spills. The spilled oil is collected and placed in containers. Since the oil is saturated with water and debris, it can't be recycled. Therefore it must be buried or destroyed. Incineration or burning *in situ* is out of the question because of air pollution restrictions. Since the oil is identified as waste oil, it fits a certain RCRA category. As such it must be tested for PCBs, pH, metals, and a number of organics. Samples must be taken to a laboratory or several laboratories, since few laboratories can run all of the required tests. Because federal regulation 49 CFR prohibits carrying flammables by air, the samples must be placed in special containers and sent by means other than common carrier, or by private auto. If all of these tests are negative, can it be buried in a local landfill by spreading and mixing it into the earth? No. A test for flammability must also be run. If the oil will ignite at less than 140°F (60°C)—and most light oils will—it is labeled hazardous and must be taken to a secure landfill. The situation with spilled chemicals is the same. Is this silly or unreasonable? Of course the answer is a resounding NO! The nation needs RCRA, and needs it now. The hazardous wastes involved in accidents can receive only minimal exemption considerations; the annual spill volume in this country is much too large for more than that. There is a problem, however, with rigidly enforcing the regulations prior to full development of all of the sanctions and accommodations envisioned by RCRA.

The disposal message is nonetheless clear to all of us. *Make every effort to reduce the final residue from any accident as much as possible.* There are numerous measures that can be taken in the initial phases of accidents to facilitate this. Those which are practical at this writing are:

1 Restriction of water use where possible
2 Immediate diking
3 Applying water blankets to keep floatables from penetrating the soil

4 Digging lined pits for quick chemical storage

5 Timely patching of tanks

6 Employing treatments that eliminate most of the liquids and water

7 Incineration where practical

8 Recovering as much of the spilled material as possible for recycling

9 Ensuring maximum use of the RRT and experts by demanding timely response to the incident

10 Keeping abreast of current technology and new developments

In the future (1981 to 1983), watch for:

- Wide use of mobile, activated-carbon-treatment units
- Carbon regenerators
- Mobile incinerators
- The use of sludges and other wastes as ingredients in concrete, asphalt, bricks, etc.
- *In situ* treatment developments

In summary, there are many critical decisions associated with cleanup—decisions that involve both technical considerations and how you in your vital role perceive them. As Chapter 7 insists, each person with decisions to make must be aware of those in similar roles who may be operating under different pressures, bias, and priorities, and who at times may overlap or duplicate effort. Those with significant input must therefore make every effort to get on-scene and work with the RRT to ensure that their input is considered. Just as important is the need for each person involved to appreciate the fact that once the hazardous substance accident has occurred, restoration of the environment will never be perfect, in spite of all their efforts. There will be variances, trade-offs and mistakes in spite of any regulations. The key to optimum results will always be to minimize the effects of the event through wise and timely participation.

part THREE

Assistance Systems

chapter
NINE

Technical Assistance

There is a tremendous amount of technical data available at every level of interest. Too often we do not know how or where to obtain them, and perhaps equally important, we often do not know what we really need. After reading Parts I and II of this book, it is obvious that there is an entire field of science dealing with hazardous substances accidents. The old ad hoc method of coping is fast giving way to a well-articulated, systematic approach. As a direct consequence, anyone having an interest in these events, practical or otherwise, must evaluate how his or her particular duty or interest fits into the overall scheme and then develop the skills and tools that will ultimately be most beneficial in carrying out that duty in concert with others. As you put your library together, try to obtain as many items as possible that pertain to your skill, and at the same time read, study, and train yourself and those working with or under you to know how that skill interfaces with the many other skills involved. One well-known spill responder said it best: There can be little doubt that the best-managed spill event is one in which, immediately subsequent to impact, each duty is taken and played in unison—different strokes, different notes, yet still a symphony.

9-1 REPORTING THE SPILL

As cited earlier, "any *owner* or *operator* in charge of a facility or vessel that discharges oil or hazardous substances in *harmful* quantities into waters of the United States" is under an obligation to *"immediately"* report the discharge as soon as he or she has knowledge of it, to the appropriate agency of the federal government. Failure to do this can subject the spillor to a year in jail and a

PUBLIC LAW 92-500

Requires Immediate Notification of the Appropriate Agency of the U.S. Govt. of Discharge of Oil or Hazardous Substances. (Sec. 311 (B) (5)) "Any Such Person Who Fails to Notify Immediately Such Agency of Such Discharge Shall, Upon Conviction, Be Fined Not More Than $10,000, or Imprisoned for Not More Than One Year, or Both."

THE NUMBER FOR REPORTING SPILLS IS:
NATIONAL RESPONSE CENTER
800-424-8802 (24 HOUR)
IF IMPRACTICAL TO REPORT TO THE ABOVE NUMBER, IN AL, FL, GA, KY, MS, NC, SC, TN CALL:
U. S. ENVIRONMENTAL PROTECTION AGENCY
404-881-4062 (24 HOUR)
OR
CALL AN APPROPRIATE U.S. COAST GUARD OFFICE IN YOUR AREA.

REPORT THE FOLLOWING INFORMATION

1. NAME, ADDRESS AND TELEPHONE NO. OF PERSON REPORTING.
2. EXACT LOCATION OF SPILL.
3. COMPANY NAME AND LOCATION.
4. MATERIAL SPILLED.
5. ESTIMATED QUANTITY.
6. SOURCE OF SPILL.
7. CAUSE OF SPILL.
8. NAME OF BODY OF WATER INVOLVED, OR NEAREST BODY OF WATER TO THE SPILL AREA.
9. ACTION TAKEN FOR CONTAINMENT AND CLEAN-UP.

Fig. 9-1 Warning placard issued by EPA.

criminal fine of $10,000, or both [The Federal Water Pollution Control Act of 1978 (Sec. 311)]. Anyone involved in such a spill situation should call:

1-800-424-8802

This 24-hour, 7-day number is operated by the U.S. Coast Guard and is toll-free. Tens of thousands of notice placards such as those shown in Figure 9-1 have been mailed to potential spillors throughout the United States in an effort to alert government and industry to the existence of this principal number and to alternatives in the event that the number is not available.

When this number is called immediately and the spill reported, the Federal liability sanction is relieved as to the spillor. Certain states also have immediate reporting requirements, so get the state laws in your area and study them.

The word *immediate* means just that; do not believe the 24-hour rumor. Reporting the spill within minutes will benefit the spillor the most in terms of total liability. Some courts have allowed more than an hour between spill and reporting, but such allowances were usually based on what was possible under the circumstances. As for the interpretation of the phrase *waters of the United States,* in the early 1970s the U.S. 6th Circuit Court of Appeals ruled in *U.S. v. Ashland* that (in the case of *that* oil spill) "all waters within the geographical definition of the United States are waters of the United States." This decision excluded underground waters. As for the word *harmful,* a recent court decision held that a visible sheen of oil could be harmful. A reportable quantity of hazardous materials is one that *may be* harmful. As a practical matter, isn't it risky *not* to report all spills?

When a spill is reported, the duty officer will have the predesignated EPA or Coast Guard response official contact the spillor within minutes. The response official will then put the spillor in touch with the appropriate state officials. As a result of these calls the spillor will receive various kinds of technical information, including where to find immediate containment and cleanup forces. The duty officer at **1-800-424-8802** is also equipped to put appropriate officials in touch with the chemical assistance offered by CHEMTREC. But *do not call this number for casual nonemergency information.* There are only limited numbers of people and lines.

9-2 TECHNICAL HOT LINES

CHEMTREC—The Chemical Transportation Emergency Center, Washington, D.C. The 24-hour hot line is **1-800-424-9300**. (In Washington, D.C., it is 887-1255.) CHEMTREC serves as a clearinghouse by providing this one 24-hour telephone number for chemical transportation emergencies. Upon receiving notification of a spill, CHEMTREC immediately contacts the shipper of the chemicals for assistance and follow-up. CHEMTREC also provides warnings and limited guidance to those at the scene of the emergency if the product can be identified by either the chemical or trade name. The

CHEMTREC system covers over 3600 items which have been submitted by manufacturers as their primary items of shipment. CHEMTREC is sponsored by the Chemical Manufacturers Association (called the Manufacturing Chemists Association prior to 1979), although nonmembers are also served. The system is not computerized. The CHEMTREC emergency telephone number is widely distributed to emergency service personnel, to carriers, and to people throughout the chemical industry, and is usually printed on bills of lading. When an emergency call is received by CHEMTREC, the person on duty obtains as much information as possible from the caller and records the essential information in writing. He or she will then give out information (as furnished by the chemical producers) on the chemical(s) reported to be involved. This information includes data on the hazards of spills, fire, or exposure. After advising the caller, the person on duty immediately telephones the shipper of the chemical, imparting the details of the situation. At this point, responsibility for further guidance passes to the shipper. CHEMTREC's function is basically to serve as the liaison between the person with the problem and the chemical shipper and/or manufacturer, on the theory that the manufacturer of the chemical or material will know the most about the product. CHEMTREC also serves as a contact point for the Chlorine Institute, the National Agricultural Chemicals Association (pesticides), and the Energy Research and Development Administration (radioactive materials). Remember! CHEMTREC is for emergency calls only!

CHLOREP—Chlorine Emergency Plan. The 24-hour hot line is **1-800-424-9300**. (In Washington, D.C., it is 887-1255.) The CHLOREP system operates through CHEMTREC, which will access CHLOREP data for you. Through the Chlorine Institute, chlorine manufacturers in the United States and Canada have established this plan to handle chlorine emergencies. This is essentially a mutual aid program, whereby the manufacturer closest to the emergency will provide technical assistance even if it involves another manufacturer's product. Upon receiving an emergency call, CHEMTREC notifies the appropriate party according to the plan. This party then contacts the emergency scene to determine whether it is necessary to send a technical team to provide assistance. Each participating manufacturer has trained personnel and equipment available for emergencies. Again, *emergency calls only!*

TEAP—Transportation Emergency Assistance Plan, Canadian Chemical Producers Association (CCPA). Hot lines are listed below by regional centers. TEAP serves a function in Canada similar to that of CHEMTREC in the United States. Canada is divided into eight geographic areas, each served by a regional control center. Depending on the location of the spill, one of these control centers is called and notified of the emergency. The functions of TEAP are to provide emergency advice, to put knowledgeable personnel (usually the manufacturer) in touch with responsible people at the emergency scene, and to see that on-scene assistance is provided if needed. When a call is received at a regional control center, the attendant enters basic information on a record sheet, obtains a callback number, and may also provide preliminary information from standard references if the name of the product is known. The attendant will immediately call one of the center's technical advisers with the preliminary information. The technical adviser will then call the accident scene to obtain as much detail as possible and, if possible, will provide additional advice on coping with the emergency. The adviser will then attempt to contact the producer. If the producer can be contacted, the adviser will turn the problem over to it as the most knowledgeable contact. If the producer cannot be reached or if distances are great, the regional control center will contact a company familiar with the product. The center is also prepared to send staff and equipment to the scene if necessary. Once contact has been established between the producer and the local authorities on the scene, the technical adviser assumes a follow-up role and notifies CCPA of the incident.

Regional Control Centers and their 24-hour telephone numbers (*for emergency use only*) include:

Hooker Chemicals Division
Vancouver, British Columbia
(604)929-3441
Region: British Columbia

Celanese Canada Ltd.
Edmonton, Alberta
(403)477-8339
Region: Prairie Provinces

Canadian Industries Ltd.
Copper Cliff, Ontario
(705)682-2881
Region: Northern Ontario

Dow Chemical of Canada, Ltd.
Sarnia, Ontario
(519)339-3711
Region: Central Ontario

Cyanamid of Canada, Ltd.
Niagara Falls, Ontario
(416)356-8310
Region: Eastern Ontario

DuPont of Canada, Ltd.
Maitland, Ontario
(613)348-3616
Region: Western Ontario

Allied Chemical Canada, Ltd.
Valleyfield, Quebec
(514)373-8330
Region: Quebec, south of St. Lawrence

Gulf Oil Canada, Ltd.
Shawinigan, Quebec
(819)537-1123
Region: Quebec, north of St. Lawrence

IRAP—Interagency Radiological Assistance Plan. Hot lines are available by contacting the U.S. Energy Research and Development Administration (ERDA) regional offices. The Interagency Radiological Assistance Plan is designed to help anyone coping with radiation emergencies to obtain technical guidance. IRAP operates through ERDA but works closely with other federal, state, military, and regional groups. In this plan, the United States is divided into eight geographical areas of responsibility, each with a regional coordinating office. Upon receiving an emergency call, the regional coordinator investigates the situation to assess the potential radioactive hazard, obtaining as much information as possible by telephone on the specifics of the situation and the type of material (e.g., from the shipping papers). Advice will be given over the phone if the potential hazard appears minimal. If the spill or leak appears serious, a technical response team will be dispatched. This team will work jointly with state personnel (civil defense, public health) whenever possible. In any case, the coordinating office will notify the appropriate state office of the radioactive spill. When the response team is dispatched, the Nuclear Regulatory Commission (NRC) is notified, especially if the spilled material is licensed. The main functions of the response team are to assess the hazard, to inform people of the hazard, and to recommend emergency actions to minimize the hazard. The responsibility for cleanup rests with the shipper or carrier (the party who has possession of the material at the time of the spill). Radiological spills are not covered either by the 1510 Plan, or in this book.

The U.S. Army Technical Escort Center Chemical Response Team. The hot-line number for this team is the 24-hour spill number of your EPA regional office. (To avoid dating this text and inconveniencing the reader, these numbers are not given here, but they can be found in local directories with little effort.) The U.S. Army Technical Escort Center maintains a 14-man alert team on standby at Aberdeen Proving Ground, Maryland, ready to respond to chemical emergencies within 2 hours. If necessary, additional personnel are available for mobilization. The team is trained and experienced in handling chemical emergencies and has at its disposal special equipment such as decontamination trucks, detection devices, and protective clothing. The team was formed primarily to respond to emergencies involving Army chemicals but has assisted other agencies such as the Coast Guard and EPA. To obtain the assistance of the escort team, contact should be made with the regional EPA office. EPA personnel will then contact the Army Operations Center. Upon receipt of each request, the Army Operations Center determines whether the specific services of the Technical Escort Center are needed. If it is determined that the emergency team will respond, intermediate commands are notified and the team is dispatched.

The National Agricultural Chemical Association (pesticides). The hot-line number is the same as that for CHEMTREC: **1-800-424-9300**. (In Washington, D.C., it is 887-1255.) Through its members, the national Agricultural Chemical Association operates a national pesticide information and response network. Its function is to provide advice and on-site assistance when the spill situation warrants it. The network operates through the CHEMTREC office. Upon receiving notification of an emergency involving a pesticide, CHEMTREC contacts the manufacturer, who will provide specific advice for the handling of the spill. If necessary, spill response teams are available on a geographical basis to assist at the emergency scene.

It is important to note that in calling any of these hot lines, you must immediately give the official receiving the call the following information:

1 Your name

2 Your present location and phone number (if you are moving around, provide a call-back number and the name of a contact)

3 Location of problem

4 Your best description of the scope of the problem (e.g., truck, train, fixed facility, how much involvement), proximity to bodies of water, and density of housing and/or people

5 Local conditions (weather, winds, etc.)
6 Shipper or manufacturer
7 Container type
8 Rail car or truck number
9 Any labeling information
10 Carrier name
11 Consignee

This information differs, of course, from that identified by the placard shown in Figure 9-1, which was designed prior to the hazardous substances era. The above list is geared to the hazardous substances accident.

9-3 TECHNICAL ASSISTANCE PERSONNEL

Federal OSC

These frequently discussed officials are located in the EPA regional offices, the U.S. Coast Guard district, and Captain of The Port or Marine Safety Offices. When a spill occurs, the Coast Guard duty official manning the 24-hour reporting number (**1-800-424-8802**) will automatically alert this official. However, for information about a prespill situation, or in case the Coast Guard number fails, you should find out and keep a current record of the regional numbers.

State spill or emergency official

The federal OSC or duty official at the regional or district level will alert the appropriate state officials. However, most states have 24-hour spill numbers. You should find out what they are and record them. Some states also have a mandatory reporting requirement; be aware of this.

Other officials and technical aids

The reporting matrix shown in Chapter 2 (Figure 2-4, page 26) is the most useful means of sorting out who may help. Contacts are made automatically by the various local, state, and federal agencies during an emergency.

The point is that *one call to 1-800-424-8802 immediately involves all of appropriate government agencies.*

The Environmental Protection Agency's Emergency Response Team

Two teams of experts (one located in Edison, New Jersey, and the other in Cincinnati, Ohio) are on call to assist the OSC in resolving technical matters whenever requested. They are available on a 24-hour basis for response and are accessed only through the federal OSC.

The U.S. Coast Guard strike teams

The Coast Guard's National Strike Force (NSF) is part of the 1510 plan. It consists of trained personnel and high-seas equipment available to assist the OSC upon request in containment and countermeasures, cleanup, mitigation and disposal, documentation, and cost and recovery, as defined in the national contingency plan. There are three Coast Guard strike teams located on the East, West, and Gulf coasts. Each strike team consists of 18 or 19 individuals, including 3 or 4 officers. Each strike team is capable of responding to a pollution incident in its area with a staff of 4 or more within 2 hours, and at full strength in 12 hours. The strike team can provide advice on ship salvage, diving, and removal techniques, and communications support and assistance. Strike force equipment, most of which is designed for air transport, consists of the following:

1 The Air Deliverable Antipollution Transfer System (ADAPTS), consisting of a pumping system to off-load stricken cargo vessels

2 Yokohama fenders, used for side protection during vessel-to-vessel cargo transfer

3 High-seas containment barrier

4 High-seas skimmer

The services of the National Strike Force are available to any federal OSC anywhere in the country.

9-4 HARD COPY TECHNICAL DATA

CHRIS Manuals, U.S. Coast Guard. This system consists of four manuals, a regional contingency plan (part of the 1510 plan), a Hazard-Assessment Computer System (HACS), and an organizational unit at the Coast Guard station. The four manuals are as follows:

Vol. 1-CG-446-1 *Condensed Guide to Chemical Hazards* contains essential information on hazardous chemicals that are shipped in large volumes by marine transportation.

Vol. 2-CG-446-2 *Hazardous Chemical Data Manual* contains detailed information on the chemical, physical, and toxicological properties of hazardous chemicals, in addition to the information in Volume 1.

Vol. 3-CG-446-3 *Hazardous Assessment Handbook* contains methods of estimating the rate and quantity of hazardous chemicals that may be released and methods for predicting the potential toxic, fire, and explosive hazards.

Vol. 4-CG-446-4 *Response Methods Handbook* contains information on existing methodology for handling spills. The Appendix to this volume contains a list of manufacturers of equipment which may be useful in a spill situation.

Volume 1, *Condensed Guide to Chemical Hazards,* is intended for use by port security personnel and others who may be first to arrive at the scene of the accident. It contains easily understood information about the hazardous nature of the chemical, assuming the chemical is identified. It is intended to assist those present to quickly determine the actions that must be taken immediately to safeguard life, property, and the environment. Volume 1 contains a list of the information needed to assess potential hazardous effects when you are using Volume 3.

Volumes 2, 3, and 4 are intended for use by the OSC's office and the regional and national response centers. Coast Guard stations, especially those in major ports, will also usually have these manuals.

Volumes 2 and 3 are designed to be used together. Volume 2, The *Hazardous Chemical Data Manual,* contains a hazard-assessment code for each chemical. This code is used in Volume 3, The *Hazard Assessment Handbook,* to select the appropriate calculation procedures for estimating the rate and quantity of hazardous chemicals that may be released under different situations. For example, procedures are provided for estimating the concentration of hazardous chemicals (both in water and in air) based on the time and distance from the spill.

Volume 4, *Response Methods Handbook,* contains descriptive and technical information on methods of spill (primarily oil) containment. This manual is intended for use by Coast Guard OSC personnel who have had some training or experience in hazard response.

The Hazard Assessment Computer System is the computerized counterpart of Volume 3. Although calculations can be performed by hand using Volume 3, the HACS permits one to make a faster, more detailed, and usually more accurate assessment of the spill situation. The HACS system is intended primarily for use by OSC personnel through Coast Guard headquarters. While the input needed for evaluation will depend on the specific accident situation and on the part of the system to be used, the following information should be supplied to Coast Guard headquarters as applicable:

Material discharged
Quantity spilled
Quantity originally in tank
Location of spill
Time of occurrence
Tank dimensions
Other cargoes or nearby chemicals
Hole diameter
River depth
River width
Stream velocity
Temperature (air)
Temperature (water)
Cloud cover (percent)

Depending on which model is to be used, other information may be needed by Coast Guard headquarters. In this case, a call-back number should be given so that headquarters personnel can request additional information if necessary.

Access to the CHRIS manuals can be obtained through the Coast Guard district office. The HACS can be accessed on an emergency basis through the regional response center, the Coast Guard district office, or directly through the Department of Transportation National Response Center at Coast Guard headquarters. A CHRIS card pertaining to one chemical is shown in Figure 9-2.

CLX | **CHLORINE**

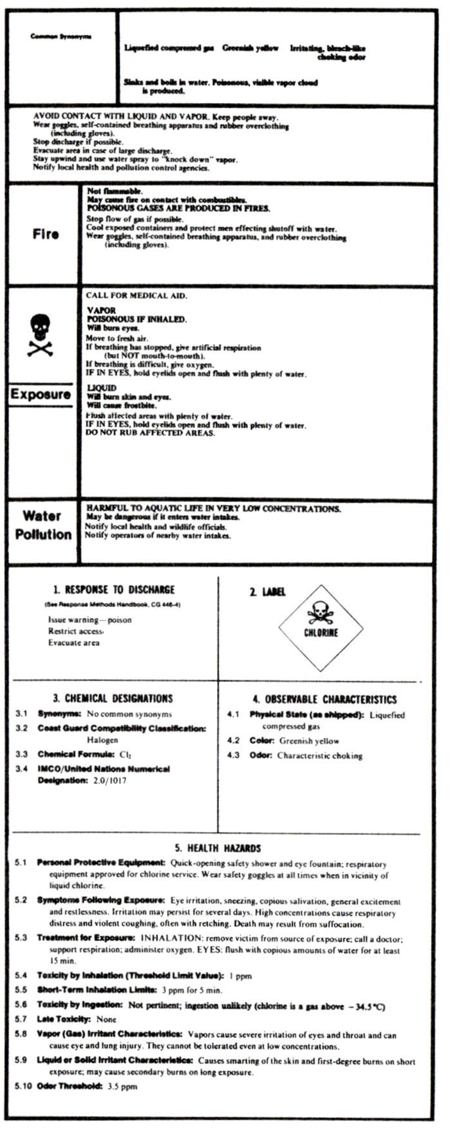

Common Synonyms

Liquefied compressed gas **Greenish yellow** **Irritating, bleach-like choking odor**

Sinks and boils in water. Poisonous, visible vapor cloud is produced.

AVOID CONTACT WITH LIQUID AND VAPOR. Keep people away.
Wear goggles, self-contained breathing apparatus and rubber overclothing (including gloves).
Stop discharge if possible.
Evacuate area in case of large discharge.
Stay upwind and use water spray to "knock down" vapor.
Notify local health and pollution control agencies.

Fire

Not flammable.
May cause fire on contact with combustibles.
POISONOUS GASES ARE PRODUCED IN FIRES.
Stop flow of gas if possible.
Cool exposed containers and protect men effecting shutoff with water.
Wear goggles, self-contained breathing apparatus, and rubber overclothing (including gloves).

Exposure

CALL FOR MEDICAL AID.

VAPOR
POISONOUS IF INHALED.
Will burn eyes.
Move to fresh air.
If breathing has stopped, give artificial respiration (but NOT mouth-to-mouth).
If breathing is difficult, give oxygen.
IF IN EYES, hold eyelids open and flush with plenty of water.

LIQUID
Will burn skin and eyes.
Will cause frostbite.
Flush affected areas with plenty of water.
IF IN EYES, hold eyelids open and flush with plenty of water.
DO NOT RUB AFFECTED AREAS.

Water Pollution

HARMFUL TO AQUATIC LIFE IN VERY LOW CONCENTRATIONS.
May be dangerous if it enters water intakes.
Notify local health and wildlife officials.
Notify operators of nearby water intakes.

1. RESPONSE TO DISCHARGE

(See Response Methods Handbook, CG 446-4)

Issue warning—poison
Restrict access.
Evacuate area

2. LABEL

CHLORINE

3. CHEMICAL DESIGNATIONS

3.1 **Synonyms:** No common synonyms
3.2 **Coast Guard Compatibility Classification:** Halogen
3.3 **Chemical Formula:** Cl_2
3.4 **IMCO/United Nations Numerical Designation:** 2.0/1017

4. OBSERVABLE CHARACTERISTICS

4.1 **Physical State (as shipped):** Liquefied compressed gas
4.2 **Color:** Greenish yellow
4.3 **Odor:** Characteristic choking

5. HEALTH HAZARDS

5.1 **Personal Protective Equipment:** Quick-opening safety shower and eye fountain; respiratory equipment approved for chlorine service. Wear safety goggles at all times when in vicinity of liquid chlorine.
5.2 **Symptoms Following Exposure:** Eye irritation, sneezing, copious salivation, general excitement and restlessness. Irritation may persist for several days. High concentrations cause respiratory distress and violent coughing, often with retching. Death may result from suffocation.
5.3 **Treatment for Exposure:** INHALATION: remove victim from source of exposure; call a doctor; support respiration; administer oxygen. EYES: flush with copious amounts of water for at least 15 min.
5.4 **Toxicity by Inhalation (Threshold Limit Value):** 1 ppm
5.5 **Short-Term Inhalation Limits:** 3 ppm for 5 min.
5.6 **Toxicity by Ingestion:** Not pertinent; ingestion unlikely (chlorine is a gas above −34.5°C)
5.7 **Late Toxicity:** None
5.8 **Vapor (Gas) Irritant Characteristics:** Vapors cause severe irritation of eyes and throat and can cause eye and lung injury. They cannot be tolerated even at low concentrations.
5.9 **Liquid or Solid Irritant Characteristics:** Causes smarting of the skin and first-degree burns on short exposure; may cause secondary burns on long exposure.
5.10 **Odor Threshold:** 3.5 ppm

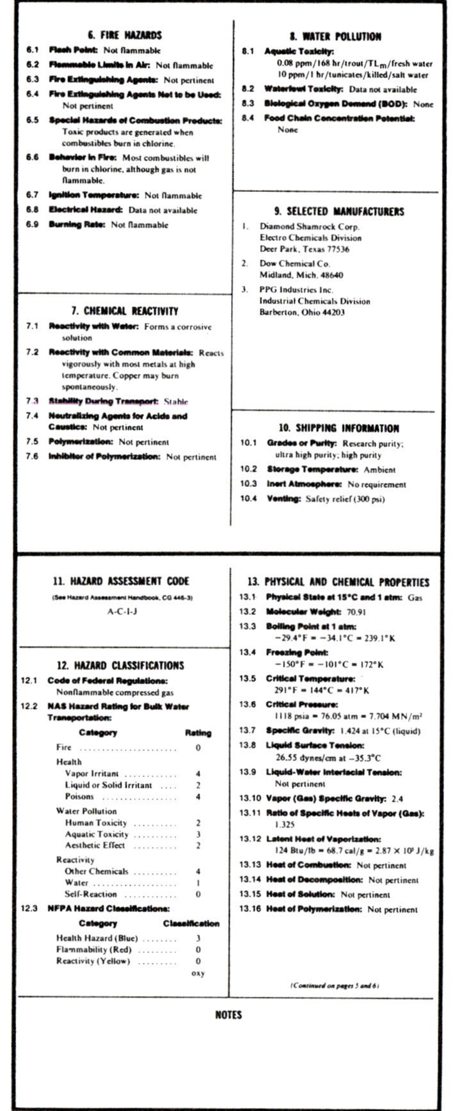

6. FIRE HAZARDS

6.1 **Flash Point:** Not flammable
6.2 **Flammable Limits in Air:** Not flammable
6.3 **Fire Extinguishing Agents:** Not pertinent
6.4 **Fire Extinguishing Agents Not to be Used:** Not pertinent
6.5 **Special Hazards of Combustion Products:** Toxic products are generated when combustibles burn in chlorine.
6.6 **Behavior in Fire:** Most combustibles will burn in chlorine, although gas is not flammable.
6.7 **Ignition Temperature:** Not flammable
6.8 **Electrical Hazard:** Data not available
6.9 **Burning Rate:** Not flammable

7. CHEMICAL REACTIVITY

7.1 **Reactivity with Water:** Forms a corrosive solution
7.2 **Reactivity with Common Materials:** Reacts vigorously with most metals at high temperature. Copper may burn spontaneously.
7.3 **Stability During Transport:** Stable
7.4 **Neutralizing Agents for Acids and Caustics:** Not pertinent
7.5 **Polymerization:** Not pertinent
7.6 **Inhibitor of Polymerization:** Not pertinent

8. WATER POLLUTION

8.1 **Aquatic Toxicity:**
0.08 ppm/168 hr/trout/TL_m/fresh water
10 ppm/1 hr/tunicates/killed/salt water
8.2 **Waterfowl Toxicity:** Data not available
8.3 **Biological Oxygen Demand (BOD):** None
8.4 **Food Chain Concentration Potential:** None

9. SELECTED MANUFACTURERS

1. Diamond Shamrock Corp.
Electro Chemicals Division
Deer Park, Texas 77536
2. Dow Chemical Co.
Midland, Mich. 48640
3. PPG Industries Inc.
Industrial Chemicals Division
Barberton, Ohio 44203

10. SHIPPING INFORMATION

10.1 **Grades or Purity:** Research purity; ultra high purity; high purity
10.2 **Storage Temperature:** Ambient
10.3 **Inert Atmosphere:** No requirement
10.4 **Venting:** Safety relief (300 psi)

11. HAZARD ASSESSMENT CODE

(See Hazard Assessment Handbook, CG 446-3)

A-C-I-J

12. HAZARD CLASSIFICATIONS

12.1 **Code of Federal Regulations:** Nonflammable compressed gas
12.2 **NAS Hazard Rating for Bulk Water Transportation:**

Category	Rating
Fire	0
Health	
Vapor Irritant	4
Liquid or Solid Irritant	2
Poisons	4
Water Pollution	
Human Toxicity	2
Aquatic Toxicity	3
Aesthetic Effect	2
Reactivity	
Other Chemicals	4
Water	1
Self-Reaction	0

12.3 **NFPA Hazard Classifications:**

Category	Classification
Health Hazard (Blue)	3
Flammability (Red)	0
Reactivity (Yellow)	0
	oxy

13. PHYSICAL AND CHEMICAL PROPERTIES

13.1 **Physical State at 15°C and 1 atm:** Gas
13.2 **Molecular Weight:** 70.91
13.3 **Boiling Point at 1 atm:** −29.4°F = −34.1°C = 239.1°K
13.4 **Freezing Point:** −150°F = −101°C = 172°K
13.5 **Critical Temperature:** 291°F = 144°C = 417°K
13.6 **Critical Pressure:** 1118 psia = 76.05 atm = 7.704 MN/m^2
13.7 **Specific Gravity:** 1.424 at 15°C (liquid)
13.8 **Liquid Surface Tension:** 26.55 dynes/cm at −35.3°C
13.9 **Liquid-Water Interfacial Tension:** Not pertinent
13.10 **Vapor (Gas) Specific Gravity:** 2.4
13.11 **Ratio of Specific Heats of Vapor (Gas):** 1.325
13.12 **Latent Heat of Vaporization:** 124 Btu/lb = 68.7 cal/g = 2.87×10^5 J/kg
13.13 **Heat of Combustion:** Not pertinent
13.14 **Heat of Decomposition:** Not pertinent
13.15 **Heat of Solution:** Not pertinent
13.16 **Heat of Polymerization:** Not pertinent

(Continued on pages 5 and 6)

NOTES

REVISED 1978

Fig. 9-2 A U.S. Coast Guard CHRIS card (vol. I).

Chem-Cards. The Chemical Manufacturers Association (CMA). Until September 1980 CMA published and updated information cards covering a number of chemicals in emergency situations. A typical Chem-Card is shown in Figure 9-3. Many of these cards are still in use.

OHMTADS—Oil and Hazardous Materials Technical Assistance Data System, EPA. Usually called TADS, this system is a computerized information retrieval file on various hazardous substances. It is generally available through the federal OSC, although a few states now access it directly. There is a TADS terminal in each EPA regional office. The material includes chemical, biological, and toxicological information on more than 1000 chemicals. Because so little is known in the scientific community about many chemicals and their behavior in the environment, these data must be carefully interpreted when they are used. A typical TADS printout is shown in Figure 9-4.

The system is presently online and available to assist in identification of a spilled material from observations (color, smell, etc.) made at the site. For each substance there are more than 100 information segments covering a wide variety of physical, chemical, biological, toxicological, and commercial data, with the greatest emphasis on the effects on water quality. TADS has a random access provision which enables the user to solve problems involving unidentified pollutants by inputting color, odor, or other physical/chemical characteristics observed on-scene. The system automatically processes each word into an inverted index file, making the word a search component of the data base. The output is displayed on the user's terminal. The user can then refine the search if necessary to narrow the list of possible materials.

In looking for characteristics of the spill to aid in identification, the 95 searchable headers should be examined to see if any of them can serve as identifiers. Of particular interest is the ability to search for chemicals by trade names.

NEELS—National Emergency Equipment Locator System. The NEELS hot-line number is **(819)997-3742**. This is an online computer system designed and operated by the Environmental Protection Service (EPS), Environment Canada. Its function is to provide information on equipment near the spill scene which is available and possibly useful. This includes containment and treatment equipment held both publicly and privately. Connection can be made with the NEELS computer system through any EPS regional office. The longitude and latitude of the spill must be entered as input, and the output must be selected from the following choices:

1 All equipment at the nearest location

2 Nearest specific type of equipment

3 Nearest particular piece of equipment

Depending on the selection, the computer prints out the location of the equipment and the name and telephone number of the person to call.

NATES—National Analysis of Trends in Emergencies System. The hot-line number is **(819)997-3742**. NATES is an online computer system designed and operated by the Canadian Environmental Protection Service (EPS), Environment

MCA CHEM-CARD — Transportation Emergency Guide

CC-53
June 1978

CHLORINE

Compressed, liquefied, greenish-yellow gas; acrid odor

IMMEDIATE HAZARDS

FIRE *Cannot catch fire, but will support combustion of certain substances.*

EXPOSURE *Gas is primarily a respiratory irritant; severe exposures can be fatal. Liquid or high concentrations of gas in contact with skin or eyes will cause local irritation or burns.*

IN CASE OF ACCIDENT

IF THIS HAPPENS

For assistance, phone
CHEMTREC
toll free, day or night
800-424-9300

DO THIS

IF THIS HAPPENS	DO THIS
SPILL or LEAK	Keep upwind from small leaks. Evacuate area in case of large leaks or tank rupture. Shut off leak if without risk. If necessary to enter spill area, wear self-contained breathing apparatus and full protective clothing including boots. Do not put water on leaking tank or on spills of liquid. Notify authorities.
FIRE	Cannot catch fire. If possible, remove vehicle from area of fire. Never use water on a chlorine leak. If no chlorine is escaping, water may be used to cool tanks that cannot be moved out of fire zone.
EXPOSURE	Remove to fresh air and call a physician at once. If not breathing, apply artificial respiration, oxygen. If breathing is difficult, administer oxygen. In case of contact with liquid, immediately flush skin or eyes with plenty of water for at least 15 minutes; remove contaminated clothing and shoes at once. Keep patient at rest.

2M-6-78

Printed in USA

Fig. 9-3 A Chem-Card by CHEMTREC (Chemical Manufacturers Association).

Canada. Its function is to provide information on how a similar spill was handled. Connection can be made with the NATES computer system through any EPS regional office. Primary input required is the type of material spilled. Output includes data on location, date, material spilled, cause, environment (including site conditions and contingency plans), cleanup (including method used), weather, agencies involved, legal actions, and cost.

```
                 FILE  1: ELEMENT    1
   (1) TECHNICAL ASSISTANCE DATA SYSTEM:  72T16637
   (2) CAS REGISTRY NO:  7782505
   (3) SIC CODE:  .; .
   (4) MATERIAL:  $$$ CHLORINE $$$
   (7) CHEMICAL FORMULA:  CL2
   (8) SPECIES IN MIXTURE:     100% CL2
   (9) COMMON USES:  ORG. CHEM PULP & PAPER INSECTICIDES INORG. CHEM
WATER & SEWAGE PHOSGENE
   (10) RAIL TRANSPORT (%):     066.
   (11) BARGE TRANSPORT (%):     013.
   (12) TRUCK TRANSPORT (%):     001.
   (13) PIPE TRANSPORT (%):    017.
   (14) CONTAINERS:  STEEL PRESSURE CYLINDERS, TANK CARS AND BARGES
   (15) GENERAL STORAGE PROCEDURES:  PROTECT AGAINST PHYSICAL DAMAGE.
SEPERATE FROM COMBUSTIBLE,ORGANIC OR EASILY OXIDIZABLE MATERIALS AND
ESPECIALLY ISOLATE FROM ACETYLENE, AMMONIA, HYDROGEN, HYDROCARBONS,
ETHER, TURPENTINE AND FINELY DIVIDED METALS. STORE OUTDOORSOR IN
WELL-VENTILATED, DETACHED OR SEGREGATED AREAS OF NONCOMBUSTIBLE
CONSTRUCTION.
   (17) PRODUCTION SITES:
   ELECTROLYTIC ALLIED CHEMICAL CORP., SYRACUSE, N.Y.; MOUNDSVILLE, W.
VA.; BATON ROUGE, LA; HOPEWELL, VA.; BRUNSWICK, GA.; WILMINGTON, N.C.;
LIVERMORE FALLS, ME.
   ALUMINUM CO. OF AMERICA, POINT COMFORT, TEXAS
   ARKLA CHEMICAL CORP., PINE BLUFF, ARK.
   BROWN CO., BERLIN, N.H.
   CHAMPION PAPERS, INC., PASADENA, TEXAS; CANTON, N.C.
   DETREX CHEMICAL INDUSTRIES, ASHTABULA, OHIO
   DIAMOND ALKALI CO., PAINESVILLE, OHIO; EDGEWOOD ARSENAL, MD;
SHEFFIELD, ALA.; DEER PARK, TEXAS; MOBILE, ALA.; DELAWARE CITY, DEL.
   DOW CHEMICAL CO., MIDLAND, MICH.; PITTSBURG, CALIF.; FREEPORT, TEXAS;
PLAQUEMINE, LA.
   E.I. DU PONT DE NEMOURS & CO., INC., NIAGARA FALLS, N. Y.; DEEPWATER
POINT, N.J.; MEMPHIS, TENN.
   EASTERN MANUFACTURING CO., SO. BREWSTER, ME.
   ECUSTA PAPER CO., PISGAH, N.C.
   ETHYL CORPORATION, BATON ROUGE, LA.; HOUSTON, TEXAS
   FMC CORP., SO. CHARLESTON, W. VA.
   FIELDS POINT MANUFACTURING CO., PROVIDENCE, R.I.
   FRONTIER CHEMICAL CO., DENVER CITY, TEXAS; WICHITA, KAN.; NEWARK,
N. J.
   GENERAL ANILINE AND FILM CORP., LINDEN, N.J.
   GEORGIA-PACIFIC CORP., COOS BAY, ORE.; BELLINGHAM, WASH.
   GULF OIL CORP., PORT ARTHUR, TEXAS
   HERCULES POWDER CO., INC., HOPEWELL, VA.; BRUNSWICK, GA.
   HOOKER CHEMICAL CORP., NIAGARA FALLS, N.Y.; TACOMA, WASH.; MONTAGUE,
MICH.; TAFT, LA.
   INTERNATIONAL MINERALS AND CHEMICAL CORP., NIAGARA FALLS, N.Y.
   JEFFERSON CHEMICAL CO., INC., PORT NECHES, TEXAS
   KAISER ALUMINUM AND CHEMICAL CORP., GRAMERCY, LA.
   KIMBERLEY-CLARK CORP., KIMBERLEY, WIS.
   MONSANTO CO., MONSANTO, ILL.; ANNISTON, ALA.
   NATIONAL DISTILLERS AND CHEMICAL CORP., ASHTABULA, OHIO; HUNTSVILLE,
```

(a)

Fig. 9-4 A TADS (Technical Assistance Data System) printout on chlorine.

```
ALA.
  NATIONAL LEAD CO., SAYREVILLE, N.J.
  NORTH CAROLINA PULP AND PAPER CO., PLYMOUTH, N.C.
  OLIN MATHIESON CHEMICAL CORP., NIAGARA FALLS, N.Y.; SALTVILLE, VA.;
MC INTOSH, ALA.; CHARLESTON, TENN.; AUGUSTA, GA.
  OXFORD PAPER CO., RUMFORD, MAINE
  PENNSALT CHEMICALS CORP., WYANDOTTE, MICH.; TACOMA, WASH.; PORTLAND,
ORE.; CALVERT CITY, KY.
  PENOBSCOT CHEMICAL FIBER CO., GREAT WORKS, MAINE
  PITTSBURGH PLATE GLASS CO., LAKE CHARLES, LA.; CORPUS CHRISTI, TEXAS;
NATRIUM, W. VA.; BARBERTON, OHIO
  STAUFFER CHEMICAL CO., NIAGARA FALLS, N.Y.; HENDERSON, NEV.;
DOMINGUEZ, CALIF.; HUNTSVILLE, ALA.; IE MOYNE, ALA.
  VELSICOL CHEMICAL CORP., MEMPHIS, TENN.
  S.D. WARREN CO., CUMBERLAND, MAINE
  WEST VIRGINIA PULP AND PAPER CO., COVINGTON, VA.; MECHANICVILLE, N.Y.
  WEYERHAEUSER TIMBER CO., LONGVIEW, WASH.
  WYANDOTTE CHEMICALS CORP., WYANDOTTE, MICH.; GEISMAR, LA.
  NOELECTROLYTIC ALLIED CHEMICAL CORP., HOPEWELL, VA.
  AMERICAN METAL CLIMAX, INC. SOUTHWEST POTASH CORP., VICKSBURG, MISS.
  HERCULES POWDER CO., BRUNSWICK, GA.
  (20) BINARY REACTANTS:  ACETYLENE, TURPENTINE, ETHER, NH3 GAS, FUEL
GAS, HYDROCARBONHYDROGEN, FINELY DIVIDED METALS, ALUMINUM
  (21) CORROSIVENESS:  HIGHLY CORROSIVE IN PRESENCE OF MOISTURE.
  (23) ANTAGONISTIC MATERIALS:  COMBINATIONS OF CHLORINE WITH AMMONIA,
ORGANIC MATTER & CYANIDES MAY BE DETRIMENTAL TO FISH LIFE. TOXICITY OF
CHLORINE TO BACTERIA INCREASES WITH DECREASING PH. PH, TEMPERATURE,
DISSOLVED OXYGEN & THE SYNERGISM & ANTAGONISM OF OTHER POLUTANTS AFFECT
TOXICITY OF FREE CL. TOWARDS FISH.
  (24) FIELD DETECTION LIMIT (PPM), TECHNIQUES, REF:     .1, CHLORINE,
BNW, 100380
  (25) LAB DETECTION LIMIT (PPM), TECHNIQUES, REF:     .01, CHLORINE,
BNW, 100381
  (26) STANDARD CODES:  EPA 311;  NFPA - 3,0,1; ICC - NONFLAMMABLE GAS,
GREEN LABEL, 150 LBS IN AN OUTSIDE CONTAINER; USCG - NONFLAMMABLE
COMPRESSED GAS; IATA - NONFLAMMABLE GAS, GREEN LABEL, NOT ACCEPTABLE
PASSENGER, 70 KG CARGO
  (27) FLAMMABILITY:  MATERIALS WILL BURN IN CHLORINE AS IN OXYGEN.
MODERATE HAZARD;
  (30) TOXIC COMBUSTION PRODUCTS:  HIGHLY TOXIC, ENTER WITH GREAT
CAUTION
  (31) EXTINGUISHING METHODS:  COOL TANKS WITH WATER SPRAY TO DECREASE
BUILDUP OF PRESSURE.DO NOT SPRAY DIRECTLY TO LEAKS AS IT WILL INCREASE
VAPORIZATION.
  (34) EXPLOSIVENESS:  SLIGHT HAZARD- FLAMMABLE GASES AND VAPORS FORM
EXPLOSIVE MIXTURES WITH CHLORINE. REACTIVE ONLY UNDER EXTREME
CONDITIONS; REACTS EXPLOSIVELY OR FORMS EXPLOSIVE COMPOUNDS WITH
ACETYLENE, TURPENTINE, ETHER, AMMONIA GAS, FUEL GAS, HYDROCARBONS,
HYDROGEN, FINELYDIVIDED METALS.
  (37) MELTING POINT (DEG C):  -101.6
  (39) BOILING POINT (DEG C):  -34.6
  (41) SOLUBILITY (PPM), 25 DEG C:  0014600.
  (43) SPECIFIC GRAVITY:  .0032
  (44) VAPOR PRESSURE (MM HG):  85.46; 151.12; 174.69; 400; 1
```

(b)

Fig. 9-4 A TADS printout on chlorine (*continued*).

```
   (45) VAPOR PRESSURE TEXT:  85.46 PSIA AT 70 DEGREES FAHRENHEIT;
151.12 PSIA AT 105 DEGREES FAHRENHEIT; 174.69 PSIA AT 115 DEGREES
FAHRENHEIT; 400 MM HG AT 25 DEGREES CELSIUS; 1 MM HG AT -118 DEGREES
CELSIUS;
   (46) VAPOR DENSITY (AIR=1):  2.44
   (50) PERSISTENCY:  CHLORINE DEMAND OF NATURAL WATERS SHOULD DEPLETE
CL2 IN A FEW DAYS.
   (57) FRESHWATER TOXICITY NUMBER (PPM):  .03; .07; .08; .0035; .15;
.008; .25; .01; .3; .35; .8; .08; 1.0; .04; 1.0; .005; 3.0; .04; 1;
.88; 2.5; .494; 10.0; .74; .5; .365; .25; .79; 2; .26; .5; .083; .083;
.005; .14; .01; .205; .261; .132; .15; .099; .082; .165; .19; .012;
.003
   (58) FRESH WATER TOXICITY TEXT
   CONC.(PPM)/EXPOS.(HR)/SPECIE/EFFECT/TEST ENV/REF
   ---------------------------------------------
   .03/ /TROUT/KILL/ /C-1
   .07-.15/96/FATHEAD MINNOW/LC50/STATIC GRAND RIVER/R-109;
   .08/168/TROUT/TLM/ /C-1
   .0035/ /YOUNG DAPHNIA/REDUCED PRODUCTION/ /R-8;
   .15/288/CARP/25%KILL/ /C-1
   .008 HOCL/96/SALMONIDS AND COARSE FISH/HARMFUL OR
LETHAL/FRESHWATERS/R-8;
   .25/5/FINGERLINGS/KILL/ /C-1
   .01/ /FISH/AVOIDANCE BEHAVIOR/ /R-8;
   .3/2/TROUT/KILLED/ /C-1
   .35/9/BROOK TROUT/MEAN SURVIVAL TIME/RESIDUAL CONCENTRATION/R-83;
   .8/.8/SMALL TROUT/KILLED/ /C-1 .8/4/SHINERS/KILLED/ /C-1
   .08/18/BROOK TROUT/MEAN SURVIVAL TIME/RESIDUAL CONCENTRATION/R-83;
   1.0/1/TROUT/KILLED/ /C-1
   .04/48/BROOK TROUT/MEAN SURVIVAL TIME/RESIDUAL CONCENTRATION/R-83;
   1.0/ /GOLDFISH/KILLED/ /C-1
   .005/24/BROOK TROUT/DEPRESSED ACTIVITY/RESIDUAL CONCENTRATION/R-83;
   3.0/24/GREEN SUNFISH/28%KILLED/ /C-1
   .04/2 MIN/BROWN TROUT/100% LETHAL/RESIDUAL CONCENTRATION/R-83;
   1/3/NAIS SPP./LETHAL/HARD/E-33
   >.88/1/YELLOW PERCH/LC50/RESIDUAL CONCENTRATION/R-83;
   2.5-5.0/0.17/OYSTERLARVAE/WITHSTAND/30C LAB/G-28
   .494/12/YELLOW PERCH/LC50/RESIDUAL CONCENTRATION/R-83;
   10.0/2/CLADOPHORA SP./DIED/ /G-31
   >.74/1/LARGEMOUTH BASS/LC50/RESIDUAL CONCENTRATION/R-83;
   .5/72/DAPHNIA/KILLED/SOFT/C-1
   .365/12/LARGEMOUTH BASS/LC50/RESIDUAL CONCENTRATION/R-83;
   .25/12/RANA PIPIENS TADPOLES/TOXIC/TEMP76F/E-187
   >.79/1/FATHEAD MINNOW/LC50/RESIDUAL CONCENTRATION/R-83;
   2/12/BULLFROG TADPOLES/LETHAL/TEMP 76F/E-187
   .26/12/FATHEAD MINNOW/LC50/RESIDUAL CONCENTRATION/R-83;
   .5/15/WHITE SUCKER/MEDIUM MORTALITY/RESIDUAL CONCENTRATION/R-83;
   .083/168/COHO SAMON/TL50/MEASURED RESIDUAL/R-83;
   .083/168/BROOK TROUT/TL50/MEASURED RESIDUAL/R-83;
   .005/ /BROOK TROUT/DEPRESSED ACTIVITY/MEASURED RESIDUAL/R-83;
   .14-.29/96/RAINBOW TROUT/TL50/MEASURED RESIDUAL/R-83;
   .01/288/RAINBOW TROUT/LETHAL/MEASURED RESIDUAL/R-83;
   .205/168/LARGEMOUTH BASS/TL50/MEASURED RESIDUAL/R-83;
   .261/168/SMALLMOUTH BASS/TL50/MEASURED RESIDUAL/R-83;
```

(c)

Fig. 9-4 A TADS printout on chlorine (*continued*).

```
  .132/168/WHITE SUCKER/TL50/MEASURED RESIDUAL/R-83;
  .15/168/WALLEYE/TL50/MEASURED RESIDUAL/R-83;
  .099/96/BLACK BULLHEAD/TL50/MEASURED RESIDUAL/R-83;
  .082-.115/168/FATHEAD MINNOW/TL50/MEASURED RESIDUAL/R-83;
  .165/ /FATHEAD MINNOW/SAFE/MEASURED RESIDUAL/R-83;
  .19/96/GOLDEN SHINER/TL50/MEASURED RESIDUAL/R-83;
  .012-.0034/ /SCUD/SAFE/MEASURED RESIDUAL/R-83;
  .003/ /DAPHNIA MAGNA/SAFE/MEASURED RESIDUAL/R-83;
  (61) SALT WATER TOXICITY NUMBER (PPM):  10; .026; 10; .024; 10; 1;
10; .01; 1
  (62) SALT WATER TOXICITY TEXT
  CONC.(PPM)/EXPOS.(HR)/SPECIE/EFFECT/TEST ENV/REF
  ------------------------------------------------
  10/4/DA/BARNACLES/KILLED/ C-1
  .026/48/PLAICE LARVAE/LD50/INCLUDES MORIBUND LARVAE/R-48;
  10/1/TUNICATES/KILLED/ /C-1
  .024/96/PLAICE LARVAE/LD50/INCLUDES MORIBUND LARVAE/R-48;
  10/1/BRYOZA/KILLED/ /C-1
  1/ /MARINE FISH/SLIGHT IRRITATION/ /C-1
  10/ /MARINE FISH/EXTREME IRRITATION/ /C-1
  .01-.05/ /OYSTERS/REDUCEDACTIVITY/ /C-1
  1/ /OYSTERS/PUMPING STOPS/ /C-1
  (63) ANIMAL TOXICITY VALUE:  15; 430; 293; 137; 800; 138
  (64) ANIMAL TOXICITY TEXT
  VALUE/TIME/SPECIES/PARAM./ROUTE/REF.
  ------------------------------------
  15 PPM/ /HMN/TCLO/INH/R-1;
  430 PPM/30 MINUTES/HMN/LC/INH/APD;
  293 PPM/1 HR/RAT/LC50/INH/R-46;
  137 PPM/1 HR/MUS/LC50/INH/R-46;
  800 PPM/30 MINUTES/DOG/LC/FNH/APD;
  138-310/1 HR/CAT/LC/INH/APD;
  (73) AQUATIC PLANTS (PPM):  0000003.
  (74) REF FOR AQUATIC PLANTS:     , C-1
  (75) IRRIGABLE PLANTS (PPM):  0000500.
  (76) REF FOR IRRIGABLE PLANTS:     , C-1
  (79) MAJOR SPECIES THREATENED:  ALL SPECIES. .46 PPM MINIMUM
CONCENTRATION CAUSING DAMAGE TO BUCKWHEAT;
  (82) INHALATION LIMIT (VALUE):  1
  (83) INHALATION LIMIT TEXT:  3 MG/M3;
  (84) IRRITATION LEVELS (VALUE):  0000015
  (85) IRRITATION LEVELS TEXT:  <
  (86) DIRECT CONTACT:  POWERFUL VESICANT, RESP..IRRITANT. PUNGENT
IRRITATING ODOR GAS AND VAPORS ARE POISONOUS. CONTACT, LIQUID-SKIN AND
EYE IRRITANT. CAN CAUSE PULMONARY EDEMA.
  (87) GENERAL SENSATION:  GOOD WARNING PROPERTIES 4 PPM CAN BE SMELLED
IN AIR, 30 PPMPRODUCED COUGHING. .314 RECOGNITION ODOR IN AIR. 50 PPM
IS DANGEROUS.
  (88) LOWER ODOR THRESHOLD (PPM):  0000003.
  (89) LOWER ODOR THRESHOLD REFERENCE:  , C-11
  (92) UPPER ODOR THRESHOLD (PPM):  0000005.
  (93) UPPER ODOR THRESHOLD REFERENCE:  , C-11
  (106) PROLONGED HUMAN CONTACT (PPM):  0001000.
  (107) REF FOR PROLONGED HUMAN CONTACT:    , C-11
  (108) PERSONAL SAFETY PRECAUTIONS:    MAC 0.35-2.0 PPM.   SKIN, EYE
AND RESPIRATORY EQUIPMENT REQUIRED.  _USE SELF-CONTAINED BREATHING
APPARATUS OF MATERIALS NOT SUSCEPTABLE TO CHLORINE ATTACK.
```

(d)

Fig. 9-4 A TADS printout on chlorine (*continued*).

```
   (109) ACUTE HAZARD LEVEL:  MOST ALGAE CONTROLLED BY .25 PPM.
INGESTION OF WATER WITH 90 MG/L (3.2 MG/KG/DAY) CAN HAVE STRONG
PHYSIOLOGICAL; 5PPM KILLED SYMURA. EFFECTS ON HUMANS.(Q-19); MINUTE
CRUSTACEA, ROTIFIERS & DIATOMS WERE KILLED BY 1PPM. .5 PPM IN SOFT
WATER KILLED DAPHNIA IN 72 HRS. LARVAE OF CHIRONOMUS WERE (100%) KILLED
BY 2.6 PPM IN 1.5 HRS; 1.3 PPMIN 3.2 HRS, 85%BY .65 PPM IN 24 HR. FRESH
WATER MUSSELS, SNAILS, & SPONGES IN COOLING SYSTEMS WERE KILLED BY 2.5
PPM STERILIZES WATER. HIGHLY TOXIC VIA INHALATION OR
INGESTION.THRESHOLD CON. FOR FISH, .02 PPM (-188)
   (110) CHRONIC HAZARD LEVEL:  UNKNOWN  FRESHWATER SHOULD NOT EXCEED
.003 PPM AND MARINE WATERS 1/10 96 HR LC50.(R-184); LONG TERM HIGH
DOSES IN RATS CAUSED IRRITATION OF UPPER DIGESTIVE TRACT.(Q-19);
   (111) DEGREE OF HAZARD TO PUBLIC HEALTH:  HIGHLY TOXIC AGENT VIA
INHALATION OR INGESTION STRONG IRRITANT.
   (112) AIR POLLUTION:  HIGH
   (113) ACTION LEVELS:    NOTIFY FIRE AND AIR AUTHORITY.   EVACUATE
AREA, ESPECIALLY RESIDENTS DOWNWIND OF SIGHT.  _ENTER WITH GREAT
CAUTION FROM UPWIND.
   (114) IN SITU AMELIORATION:  DECHLORINATE WITH SODIUM THIOSULFATE.
CARBON IS EFFECTIVE IN REMOVING CHLORINE.
   (115) BEACH AND SHORE RESTORATION:  WASH WITH SODIUM THIOSULFATE
SOLUTION.
   (116) AVAILABILITY OF COUNTERMEASURE MATERIALS:    SODIUM
THIOSULFATE-PHOTOGRAPHY SHOPS, DYE MANUFACTURERS CARBON - WATER
TREATMENT PLANTS, SUGAR REFINERIES
   (117) DISPOSAL METHODS:  ADD TO LARGE VOLUME OF CONENTRATED REDUCER
SOLUTION (HYPO, ABISULFITE, OR A FERROUS SALT AND ACIDIFY WITH
3M-H2SO4). WHEN REDUCTION IS COMPLETE, ADD SODA ASH OR DILUTE HCL TO
NEUTRALIZE. ROUTE TO SEWAGE PLANT.
   (118) DISPOSAL NOTIFICATIUN:    LOCAL SEWAGE AUTHORITY
   (119) INDUSTRIAL FOULING POTENTIAL:  IN FOOD-PROCESSING
INDUSTRIES-CHLORINE MAY CAUSE TASTES IN CANNED OR FROZEN PRODUCTS OR
MAY BE DETRIMENTAL TO CORRODINGCANS. CHLORINE IN WATER USED FOR
METAL-PLATING BATHS WILL AFFECT THE SMOOTHNESS OR BRIGHTNESS OF THE
DEPOSITS. RESIDUAL CHLORINE SHOULD BE 3 PPM FOR HIGH-GRADE PAPER & 8
PPM FOR LOWER-GRADE PRODUCTS. MAY BE CORROSIVE TO PIPING AND EQUIPMENT.
   (121) MAJOR WATER USES THREATENED:  ALL USES.
   (122) PROBABLE LOCATION AND STATE OF MATERIAL:  GREEN-YELLOW GAS.
HEAVIER THAN AIR, WILL CLING TO GROUND. LIQUID AS SHIPPED VAPORIZES
RAPIDLY. WATER ABSORPTION SIGNIFICCANT ONLY FOR SMALL SPILLS. LEAK RATE
FROM CONTAINERS ACCELERATES DUE TO CORROSION. LIQUID SPILLS FLOAT ON
SURFACE BUOYED BY BUBBLES THAT EVOLVE. DISSOLUTION IS QUITE COMPLETE
FOR SPILLS MORE THAN 4.5 FEET BELOW THE SURFACE DURING THE FIRST FEW
HOURS IF LEAK IS SMALL. THEN AN ATMOSPHERIC PLUME DEVELOPS.
   (124) WATER CHEMISTRY:  CHLORINE HYDROLYZES IN WATER TO PRODUCE
HYPOCHLOROUS ACID. THE ACID IN TURN DISSOCIATES SUCH THAT AT PH 6, 96%
IS PRESENT IN THE NONIONIC HOCL FORM AND AT PH6 3%. AT 5 DEG C .004 PPM
HOCL RESULTS FROM .004 PPM CL2 AT PH 6, .005 PPM CL2 AT PH 7, .011 PPM
CL2 AT PH 8 AND .075 PPM AT PH 9. AT 25 DEG C .004 PPM HOCL RESULTS
FROM .004 PPM CL2 AT PH 6, .005 PPM AT PH 7, .016 PPM AT PH 8, AND .121
PPM AT PH 9. WATERS CONTAINING ORGANIC AND OXIDIZABLE INORGANIC MATTER
DISPLAY A CHLORINE DEMAND WHICH LEADS TO REDUCTION TO CHLORIDE.
CHLORINE REACTS WITH AMMONIA TO FORM TOXIC CHLORAMINES WITH A LONG
RESIDUAL LIVES.
   (125) COLOR IN WATER:  GREEN;
   (126) ADEQUACY OF DATA:  GOOD.
ENTER:
```

(e)

Fig. 9-4 A TADS printout on chlorine (*continued*).

9-5 REFERENCE BOOKS AND GUIDES*

Select for your collection, in addition to the laws and regulations appropriate for your duty, any of the following. Keep in mind that besides being expensive, many of these documents may be out of print.

List A: General Sources

1 *Manual for Control of Hazardous Materials Spills,* U.S. Environmental Protection Agency, Office of Water and Hazardous Materials, Washington, DC 20400.

2 *CHRIS Manual,* vols. 1–4 (CG-446-1-4), U.S. Coast Guard, Washington, DC 20402.

3 *Chem-Card Manuals,* Chemical Manufacturers Association, 1825 Connecticut Ave. NW, Washington, DC 20009.

4 *Your regional contingency plan,* U.S. Environmental Protection Agency, regional environmental emergency branch, regional office (for inland); U.S. Coast Guard district office (for coastal).

5 Regulations for shipping hazardous materials:

Code of Federal Regulations, Title 49; Transportation, pts. 170–189, U.S. Department of Transportation, Office of Hazardous Materials, Washington, DC 20590.

Hazardous Materials Transportation Kit, U.S. Department of Transportation, Research and Special Programs Administration, Materials Transportation Bureau, Washington, DC 20590.

Federal Aviation Regulations, vol. 6, pt. 103, U.S. Department of Transportation, Federal Aviation Administration, Washington, DC 20553.

Official Air Transport Restricted Articles, Tariff No. 6-D, pt. 82, U.S. Department of Transportation, Civil Aeronautics Board, Washington, DC 20428.

6 *EPA Field Detection and Danger Assessment Manual for Oil and Hazardous Material Spills,* U.S. Environmental Protection Agency, Office of Water and Hazardous Materials, Washington, DC 20400.

7 Sax, Irving N.: *Dangerous Properties of Industrial Materials,* Van Nostrand Reinhold Company, New York, 1975.

8 *Chemical Transportation and Handling Guide,* Railroad Systems and Management Association, P.O. Box 330, Ocean City, NJ 08226, 1972.

9 *Laboratory Waste Disposal Manual,* Chemical Manufacturers Association, 1825 Connecticut Ave. NW, Washington, DC 20009.

10 *Recommended Methods of Reduction, Neutralization, Recovery or Disposal of Hazardous Waste,* vols. 1–16 (prepared by TRW Systems Group). U.S. Department of Commerce, National Technical Information Service, Springfield, VA 22151.

11 Hazardous chemicals data, National Fire Protection Association, 470 Atlantic Avenue, Boston, MA 02110.

12 Bennett, Gary F., Frank Feates, and Ira Wilder: *Handbook of Hazardous Materials,* McGraw-Hill Book Company, New York. In preparation.

* An addendum to this section is on page 172, at the end of Part Three.

13 Your local contingency plan, sheriff's department, fire department. If it doesn't exist, force the issue.

14 Your state contingency plan, state pollution control or state civil defense office.

Those who have a more technical interest in the field or wish to have a more complete library, may consider the following material:

List B

1 Milsom, M., et al., eds.: *The Merck Index,* 9th ed., Merck & Co., Inc., Rahway, N.J., 1976.

2 Weast, Robert C., ed.: *Handbook of Chemistry and Physics,* 60th ed., CRC Press, Boca Raton, Florida, 1979.

3 Dean, John A., ed.: *Lange's Handbook of Chemistry,* 12th ed., McGraw-Hill Book Company, New York, 1979.

4 *Behavior of Organic Chemicals in the Aquatic Environment,* pt. 1, *A Literature Critique,* Manufacturing Chemists Association.* Washington, D.C., 1968.

5 *Behavior of Organic Chemicals in the Aquatic Environment,* pt. 2, *Behavior in Dilute Solutions,* Manufacturing Chemists Association, Washington, D.C., 1968.

6 *1963 Census of Manufacturers—Location of Manufacturing Plants by Industry, County, and Employment Size*

7 *Chemical Data Guide for Bulk Shipment by Water,* U.S. Coast Guard, 1966.

8 Perry, John H., et al., eds.: *Chemical Engineers' Handbook,* 5th ed., McGraw-Hill Book Company, New York, 1973.

9 *Chemical Safety Data Sheets* (SD-1–SD-96), Chemical Manufacturers Association, Washington, DC 20009.

10 Sunshine, L., ed.: *Handbook of Analytical Toxicology,* Chemical Rubber Company, Cleveland, Ohio,† 1969.

11 *Mineral Facts and Problems,* U.S. Bureau of Mines Bulletin 630, Washington, DC 20241, 1965.

12 Morrison, R. T., and R. N. Boyd: *Organic Chemistry,* 3d ed., Allyn and Bacon, Boston, 1973.

13 *Orsanco Quality Monitor* (Ohio River Sanitation Commission, Cincinnati), July, 1970.

14 *The Pesticide Review,* U.S. Department of Agriculture, Washington, DC 20251, 1970.

15 *Hygienic Guide Series,* American Industrial Hygiene Association, Akron, Ohio.

16 Pesticide Poisoning of Pond Lake, Ohio, Investigation and Resolution (study for the EPA, done by Fyckman, Edgerly, Tomlinson and Assoc., Inc.); can be obtained from U.S. Environmental Protection Agency Office of Public Affairs, Washington, DC 20460.

17 *Proceedings of Conference on Hazardous Cargoes,* U.S. Coast Guard, Washington, DC 20593, July 1970.

* Now called Chemical Manufacturers Association.

† Now the CRC Press, Boca Raton, Florida.

18 *Proceedings of the 1972 National Conference on Control of Hazardous Material Spills,* University of Houston, Texas, (and subsequent proceedings 1974, 1976, 1978), U.S. Environmental Protection Agency, Washington, DC 20460.

19 *Spill Prevention Techniques for Hazardous Polluting Substances,* Arthur D. Little Company, Cambridge, MA, for U.S. Environmental Protection Agency, Washington, DC 20460, 1971.

20 *Standard Methods for the Examination of Water and Wastewater,* American Public Health Association, American Public Water Works, and Water Pollution Control Federation, current edition.

21 McKee, J. E., and H. W. Wolf: *Water Quality Criteria,* The Resources Agency of California, State Water Quality Control Board, Sacramento, CA 95814, 1963.

22 *Water Quality Criteria—Report of the National Technical Advisory Committee to the Secretary of the Interior,* Federal Water Pollution Control Authority, Washington, DC, April 1, 1968.

23 Olson, T. A., and R. J. Burgess: *Pollution and Marine Ecology,* Wiley-Interscience, New York, 1967.

24 Railroad Accident Report, Southern Railway Company Train 154, Derailment with Fire and Explosion, Laurel, Miss., January 25, 1969.

25 *Waterborne Commerce of the United States,* pts. 1–5, U.S. Corps of Engineers, 1968. Write to: Department of The Army Office Chief of Engineers Publications Depot 890 S. Puckett St. Alexandria, VA 22304.

26 *Dangerous Articles Emergency Guide,* Bureau of Explosives and Association of American Railroads, Washington, DC.

27 *Explosives and Other Dangerous Articles,* Bureau of Explosives and Association of American Railroads, Washington, DC.

28 Bahme, C. W.: *Fire Protection for Chemicals,* National Fire Protection Association, Boston.

9-6 WHAT INFORMATION DO YOU REALLY NEED?

Many of the manuals listed above, even if available, are going to be difficult to locate. Because the demand for this type of literature has been small, the printings have been limited. Also, the scientific community is still struggling with the problem of how and where to collect this kind of literature so it can be conveniently located and ordered. Certainly, if the demand for these materials is great enough, there will be justification for reprinting and also for an organization to round up and maintain the literature developed. Finally, material on precisely how to handle the various chemicals (step-by-step methodologies) is lacking, and books on managing the entire event are nonexistent.

Data retrieval systems such as OHMTADS are available to the situation at any time. In this particular system, scientific interpretation is difficult, and the set is too bulky and costly to obtain for office use. Actually only the OSC,

SOSC, and certain scientific support specialists really need this. Just be aware that these systems are available to you 24 hours a day.

Again, try to develop a library that is suited to your duty and expertise. With the spill response scenario in mind as well as the various roles relating to cleanup phases (Chapters 3 and 7), some conclusions can be drawn as to what you really need. The following are suggestions for literature appropriate to duty categories:

Federal OSC

- The laws in Chapter 1
- OHMTADS access
- All hot lines (Sections 9-1 and 9-2)
- *CHRIS Manuals, Chem-Cards,* and *OHMTADS* access (Section 9-4)
- All references in lists A and B in (Section 9-5)

RRT Members

- All hot lines (Sections 9-1 and 9-2)
- Items 4, 13, and 14 from list A (Section 9-5)
- Your selections from list B (Section 9-5)

State On-Scene Coordinator (SOSC)

- The laws in Chapter 1
- All hot lines, (Sections 9-1 and 9-2)
- Items 1, 4, 12, 13, and 14 from list A (Section 9-5)
- All references in list B (Section 9-5)

Local On-Scene Coordinator (LOSC)

- The laws in Chapter 1
- All hot lines, (Sections 9-1 and 9-2)
- Items 2, 3, 4, 7, 13, and 14 from list A (Section 9-5)
- All references from list B (Section 9-5), especially items 6, 26, 27, and 28
- Local and state contingency plans

National Civil Defense (FEMA)

- Same as for SOSC

State Civil Defense

- Same as for LOSC plus item 12 from list A (Section 9-5)

Local Civil Defense

- All hot lines (Sections 9-1 and 9-2)
- Items 3, 4, 13, and 14 from list A (Section 9-5)
- Items 28, 29, and 30 from list B (Section 9-5)

Municipal, County, and Metropolitan Fire Departments

- All hot lines (Sections 9-1 and 9-2)
- Items 2, 3, 4, 13, and 14 from list A (Section 9-5)
- Items 25, 28, 29, and 30 from list B (Section 9-5)
- Local and state contingency plans

Fire Marshal

- All hot lines (Sections 9-1 and 9-2)
- Items 2, 3, 4, 13, and 14 from list A (Section 9-5)
- Items 6, 9, 26, 27, and 28 from list B (Section 9-5)

Volunteer Fire Departments

- All hot lines (Sections 9-1 and 9-2)
- Items 3, 4, and 14 from list A (Section 9-5)
- Items 26, 27, and 28 from list B (Section 9-5)

Sheriff

- All hot lines (Sections 9-1 and 9-2)
- Items 3, 4, 13, and 14 from list A (Section 9-5)
- Item 27 from list B (Section 9-5)

State Trooper, Highway Patrol

- All hot lines (Sections 9-1 and 9-2)
- Items 3, 4, 13, and 14 from list A (Section 9-5)

Mayor, County Commissioner, County Judge

- Items 4, 13, and 14 from list A (Section 9-5)

Red Cross, Salvation Army

- Items 4 and 14 from list A (Section 9-5)

Emergency Medical Teams

- Items 4 and 14 from list A (Section 9-5)

Industry (Users, Haulers, Manufacturers)

- All laws in Chapter 1
- All hot lines (Sections 9-1 and 9-2)
- Items 2, 3, 4, 5, 13, and 14 from list A (Section 9-5)
- Selected references from list B (Section 9-5)

Scientific, Research, and Academic Interests

- All laws in Chapter 1
- Specialized articles (Sections 9-1 and 9-2)

Cleanup Contractors

- Items 2, 3, 4, 13, and 14 from list A (Section 9-5)
- Selected references from list B (Section 9-5)

Mutual Aid Cooperatives

- All laws in Chapter 1
- All hot lines (Sections 9-1 and 9-2)
- Items 2, 3, 4, 13, and 14 from list A (Section 9-5)
- Selected references from list B (Section 9-5)
- *How to Form an Oil Spill Cooperative, North Carolina Style,* North Carolina Oil Jobbers Association, P.O. Box 30519, Raleigh, NC 27612, Attention: Mr. William L. Kemp, Jr.

chapter
TEN

Training

10-1 TRAINING AVAILABLE TODAY

In the specific context of hazardous substance accidents and cleanup, there is very little training available in the United States today. It is true that many fire training schools have expanded their curricula to include (in varying degrees) chemical fires, and many states have begun to set up courses on hands-on methods of dealing with chemical incidents. There are also a few national-level training courses that go further into planning, chemistry, toxicology, biology, and safety. But there is still not enough comprehensive training available to satisfy the growing need, and too often the training that is available is not well publicized.

Fire and General Disaster Training

Few groups (outside military demolition teams) have a better-developed, grass roots training system than those involved in fire training. The fire marshal's office or the state civil defense director's office in any state can put those with legitimate needs in touch with excellent training in fire control, rescue, and disaster management. Such training is designed to cover structure entry, fire isolation, explosions, various types of foam application, evacuation, and familiarity with personnel safety equipment. Many fire training courses are now becoming more concerned with chemical and oil fires. Civil defense and other agencies are conducting training in similar areas as well as organizing field and public-participation exercises for action and evacuation in the event of disasters such as air crashes, nuclear attack, riots, natural disasters, and in some cases, chemical incidents. If your duty lies in these areas, you may wish to become familiar with training availability by contacting the state fire marshal's office, the state civil defense office, or the state department of emergency services.

Oil Spills

As this country developed a comprehensive management approach to oil spills during the 1970s, certain aspects of fire control were by necessity built into the training programs. Almost all state-level fire training contains some aspect of oil containment and control as well as firefighting techniques, but there are also several courses available that combine management and spill-planning concepts with a hands-on approach. One such course is:

Oil Spill Control Course
Oil and Hazardous Material Control Training Division
Texas Engineering Extension Service
Texas A & M University System
College Station, TX 77843

Those who specialize in the management aspects of oil spill emergencies may be interested in a course taught by the U.S. Coast Guard. Designed for OSCs, this course offers training appropriate to both oil spill planning and response. Write or call:

OSC/RRT Training Program
U.S. Coast Guard Marine Environment Systems School
Yorktown, VA 23690
(804)898-3500

The course offered by the National Spill Control School presents an overview of oil spill control problems and focuses on available equipment and techniques for organizing oil spill cleanups in all environments. Cleanup practices used in most areas of the U.S. are detailed, along with suggestions of preferred methods for cleanup preparation in different environments. For information write to:

National Spill Control School
Corpus Christi State University
6300 Ocean Drive
Corpus Christi, TX 78412

Hazardous Substances Training

There is some training available for those who respond to hazardous substance accidents. These programs are limited by the duty scope of the sponsoring organization but could be selected as parts of your overall program. Be sure to ask questions about the course descriptions and to examine the faculty and your own goals prior to enrolling.

The U.S. Environmental Protection Agency periodically conducts (through their regional training office or the regional laboratory) seminars covering some aspects of hazardous substances and toxic materials in the environment. Call or write the appropriate EPA regional office and inquire.

The U.S. Coast Guard conducts a training course that should be of interest to spill responders with a strong safety orientation. Contact:

Hazardous Chemical Course
U.S. Coast Guard Training Center
Yorktown, VA 23690
(804)898-3500

The Toxic Substance Control Laboratory at Vanderbilt University in conjunction with The Environmental Resources Group, IMS America, Ltd. conducts a National Hazardous Materials Training Course monthly in various major cities throughout the United States. Originally developed in conjunction with the U.S. Environmental Protection Agency, this seminar has been attended by over 800 participants from industry and government, including representatives from IBM, General Motors, Monsanto, U.S. Steel, Allied Chemical, TVA, U.S. EPA, U.S. Air Force, U.S. Coast Guard, and state environmental regulatory agencies, as well as from foreign countries. The course is designed to provide participants with a basic, technical overview of the newly emerging field of hazardous materials control. Participants receive a 975-page training manual with supplemental materials on a broad range of related topics, including chemistry, transportation, health hazards, emergency response, protective equipment, and disposal. The course has been designed to achieve the following objectives:

1 To provide a clearer understanding of the effects of hazardous materials on the environment and human health.

2 To increase the participants' ability to manage hazardous materials effectively and safely in normal operations and in spills and other emergencies and to comply with federal and state laws.

3 To increase the participants' knowledge of the multidisciplinary aspects of hazardous materials control, including state-of-the-art updates in chemistry, toxicology, laws and regulations, engineering, transportation, protective equipment, and disposal.

Information may be obtained by writing:

Toxic Substance Control Laboratory
Vanderbilt Medical Center
Nashville, TN 37232
Attention: Dr. R. D. Harbison

or

Dr. Thomas H. F. Smith, Director
Environmental Resources Group
IMS America, Ltd.
Ambler, PA 19002

The National Hazardous Control Institute conducts a periodic course: Hazardous Materials Control. This course covers such areas as:

1 Hazardous materials engineering
2 Hazardous health policies
3 Identification of hazardous materials
4 Sampling, measuring, and monitoring

For information contact:

National Hazardous Control Institute
P.O. Box 133
Stanton, NJ 08885

The Chemical Manufacturers Association sponsors short seminars under the name of Chemical Emergency Transportation Response. The focus of these 2-day workshop courses concerns on-scene activities in transportation-related spills. Contact:

Chemical Manufacturers Association
1825 Connecticut Ave. NW
Washington, DC 20009
Attention: Mr. John C. Zercher (202)887-1255

The Center for Professional Advancement holds a 3-day course in case histories, chemical identification and properties, waste disposal, and contingency planning. Write:

The Center for Professional Advancement
P.O. Box H
East Brunswick, NJ 08816
(201)249-1400

The National Fire Protection Association (together with the U.S. Department of Transportation) sponsors a 5-day course called Handling Hazardous Materials Transportation Emergencies. Basic topics are:

1 Response techniques
2 General hazards
3 Coordination
4 Operating procedures

Address:

National Fire Protection Association
470 Atlantic Avenue
Boston, MA 02210
Telex 94-0720 or (617)482-8755

J.T. Baker Chemical Company offers a 2-day course in flammable liquids, explosions, protective equipment, and waste disposal. Contact:

J.T. Baker Chemical Company
Office of Safety Training
Phillipsburg, NJ 08860
(201)454-2500

The State of Tennessee, Office of Civil Defense, conducts one of the most intensive hands-on, "first responder" courses in the country. This 6-week, rigid work course teaches many of the defense mechanisms associated with chemical spills. Of key importance to firefighters are the emphasis on containing liquids and minimizing the use of water, and the major focus on recognizing the chemicals that are sensitive to water. This course, designed and funded by the State of Tennessee, is naturally available to state residents first. Extra slots are then open to others on a first-come basis. You may write:

The State of Tennessee
Office of Civil Defense
3401 Sidco Drive
Nashville, TN 37204

Contingency Planning Guide and Training Course

In order to aid state and local officials in developing and improving contingency plans for hazardous substances spills, EPA and the Federal Emergency Management Agency (FEMA) have sponsored the development of a planning guide and checklist, *Preparing for Environmental Emergencies.* This guide primarily addresses the critical first step—the preparation of the plan itself—and provides instruction and criteria for deciding the type of plan needed, how to go about preparing it, what to include, and how to coordinate and interface with other existing plans, particularly when events may reach disaster proportions. A 2-day (or 4-evening) training course has also been developed to cover this same area and is widely available. For information, contact either:

Division of Oil and Special Material Control
Spill Prevention & Control Branch (WH-548)
Office of Water Program Operations
U.S. Environmental Protection Agency
401 M Street SW
Washington, DC 20460

or:

FEMA
Directorate for Plans and Preparedness
Attention: PP-RADEF
Washington, DC 20472

A home study version of this course, including cassette tapes, student manuals, and supplementary reading, is also available. Contact:

Rockwell International
Environmental Monitoring & Services Center
2421 West Hillcrest Drive
Newbury Park, CA 91320

10-2 WHAT KIND OF TRAINING IS NEEDED?

Each course mentioned in Section 10-1 is vital in some specific area. By evaluating your specific duty and predicting the role you may play in an incident, you can select the particular courses that are most valuable for you and your team.

If you have read the first five chapters of this book, however, it will be obvious that none of these courses will make you a response person in the complete sense. Missing from all the training courses mentioned is the complicated, time-consuming treatment of overall accident management. For example, how do you fit in the *total* picture? It does you no good to be able to patch the car, contain the liquid, and recover the soil unless you know where to take the material recovered, or where and why you cannot take it. Naturally you cannot be expected to learn it all. We have said many times that *no one person can be totally in charge,* but until you know the whole management scenario, you cannot predict the various other activities that will ultimately affect your function. Isn't it important that the fire chief, the sheriff, etc., know what an OSC is and why he is there? Isn't it also vital that the civil defense director be aware of the national, regional, state, and local contingency plans? How can all of this interaction be effective, even with the best training, until that training shows how it all fits together?

Contingency Planning Training

Some day in the near future such a course should be developed, and it must be included in every response person's academic background. It is true that several of the courses listed in Section 10-1 involve contingency planning to some extent, but none go far enough. A course on how to manage a hazardous substance accident would take at least 40 to 80 classroom hours, and this would exclude all technical information. The management concept lacks flair, but it is vital.

A National Training Facility for Hazardous Substances

There is no such facility, but there should be. A central national facility with perhaps 100 acres of training grounds, a short stream with variable flow capabilities, a small pond with a wave simulator, a chemical and biological laboratory, small, foliaged test areas, classical fire training areas, a waste disposal incinerator, and a small, secure landfill would meet a wide range of needs.

Figure 10-1 is a sketch of such a dream. Consider the training possibilities afforded by this facility. Packaged programs such as a warehouse fire or a train or truck wreck, from time zero until final disposal of the hazardous wastes, could all be run on this one facility. Future trainers could be trained and then teach here.

Academic Training

At least one major university in the Southeast is considering offering a fully accredited, graduate-level course in managing hazardous accidents. The problem, of course, is obtaining adequate text material.

Engineering schools throughout the United States have seriously modified their approach to the time-honored field of sanitary engineering. In the past 10 years, many schools have introduced degree programs in environmental engineering to supplement the sanitary field. Conceptual teaching has developed into a more detailed study of the ecological systems and the degradation of our natural resources without quantifying damages in terms of public health; the study of various forms of planning has been added to that of strict technical theories. We know that emergencies traumatize both people and the environment, and we are learning that the long-term effects may be more dramatic than the chronic effects with which we and/or the environment are most familiar. We are teaching classical chemistry, biology, toxicology, management, and government in an effort to satisfy an historic need for such talent, but there is a growing market for specialists who can apply this training to emergency situations. Legislation is pending before the Congress that if passed will create slots for several thousand people to respond to and control the hazardous substance nightmare in which we find ourselves. The immediate result of such legislation will be corresponding legislative activity throughout state and local governments as well as throughout industry. Where will all this talent come from? Much of it is potentially available now with perhaps only minimal additional training, but where will this minimal additional training take place? In the 1960s this country proved itself affluent enough to send a man to the moon and back; certainly we can set aside sufficient funds to manage this growing problem that affects all of us to one degree or another.

"First Responder" Training

In the United States, there is probably more training available to those who must be involved in early-response (phases 1 and 2) efforts than to those in any other emergency area. The courses outlined in Section 10-1 relate very well to this need. Unfortunately, there are simply not enough of them avail-

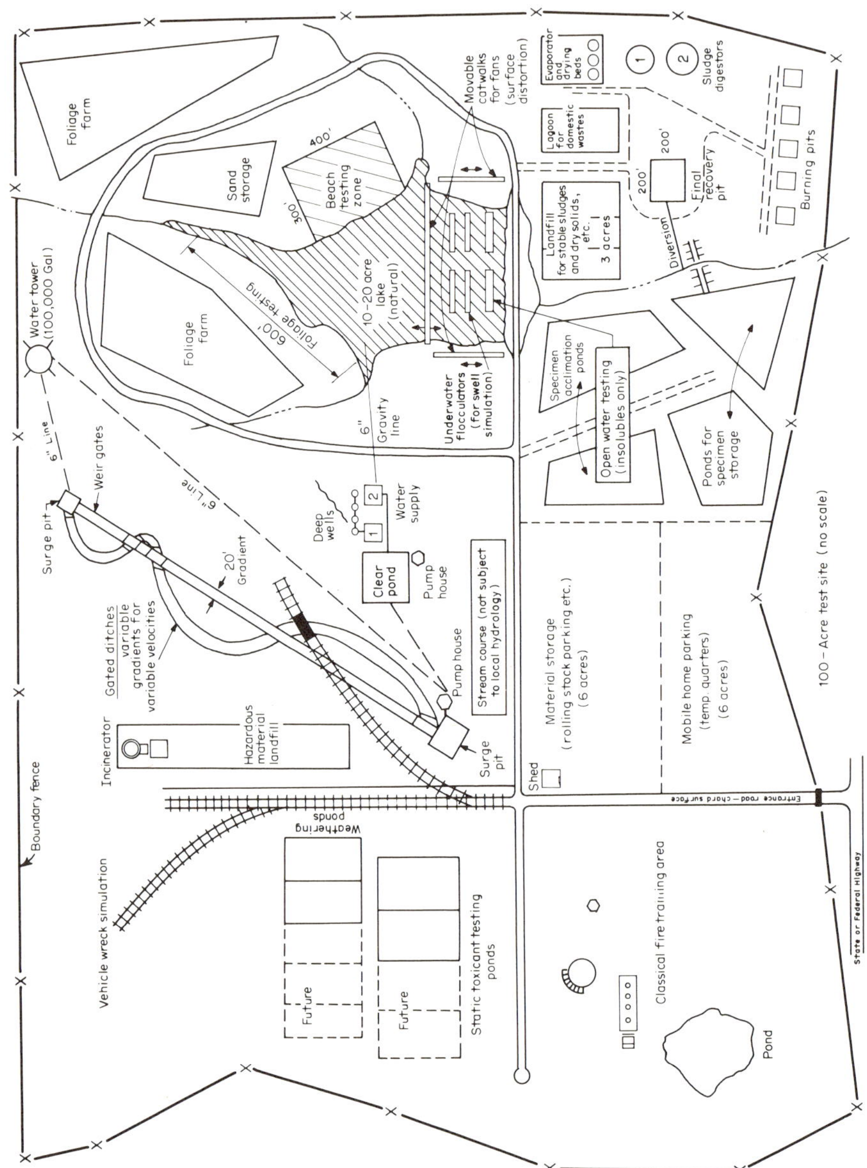

Fig. 10-1 Concept for a national hazardous substance spill training facility.

DOT HAZARDOUS MATERIALS WARNING PLACARDS

PLACARDING ANY QUANTITY—

MOTOR VEHICLES, FREIGHT CONTAINERS AND RAIL CARS

Placard motor vehicles, freight containers, and rail cars containing "any quantity" of hazardous materials listed in TABLE 1.

TABLE 1

HAZARDOUS MATERIAL CLASSED OR DESCRIBED AS	PLACARDS
Class A explosives	EXPLOSIVES A
Class B explosives	EXPLOSIVES B
Poison A	POISON GAS
Flammable solid (DANGEROUS WHEN WET label only)	FLAMMABLE SOLID W
Radioactive material	RADIOACTIVE
Radioactive material:	
Uranium hexafluoride, fissile (containing more than 0.7 pct U^{235})	RADIOACTIVE AND CORROSIVE
Uranium hexafluoride, low specific activity (containing 0.7 pct. or less U^{235})	RADIOACTIVE AND CORROSIVE

EXPLOSIVES A

EXPLOSIVES B

POISON GAS 2

FLAMMABLE SOLID

RADIOACTIVE 7

YELLOW III labeled packagings only.

For Uranium Hexafluoride, see Sec. 172.504(a) and TABLE 1.

RAIL PLACARDS

EXPLOSIVES A

POISON GAS 2

EMPTY POISON GAS 2

SQUARE BACKGROUND FOR RAIL SHIPMENTS – Each EXPLOSIVE A placard, POISON GAS placard and POISON GAS – EMPTY placard affixed to a rail car must be placed on a square background measuring 14¼ inches on each side with a black border extending to 15½ inches on each side (illustrated in above chart). (See Sec. 172.510(a) and 172.527(a)).

OTHER PLACARDING REQUIREMENTS

MOTOR VEHICLES, RAIL CARS AND FREIGHT CONTAINERS

1. Placard motor vehicles and freight containers containing 1,000 pounds or more gross weight of hazardous materials classes listed in TABLE 2.
2. Placard any quantity of hazardous materials classes listed in TABLES 1 and 2 when offered for transportation by air or water.
3. Placard rail cars containing any quantity of hazardous materials classes listed in TABLE 2 except when less than 1,000 pounds gross weight of hazardous materials is transported in TOFC (Trailer on flat car) or COFC (Container on flat car) service.

TABLE 2

HAZARDOUS MATERIAL CLASSED OR DESCRIBED AS	PLACARDS
Class C explosives	FLAMMABLE
Nonflammable gas	NONFLAMMABLE GAS
Nonflammable gas (Chlorine)	CHLORINE
Nonflammable gas (Fluorine)	POISON
Nonflammable gas (Oxygen, pressurized liquid)	OXYGEN
Flammable gas	FLAMMABLE GAS
Combustible liquid	COMBUSTIBLE
Flammable liquid	FLAMMABLE
Flammable solid	FLAMMABLE SOLID
Oxidizer	OXIDIZER
Organic peroxide	ORGANIC PEROXIDE
Poison B	POISON
Corrosive material	CORROSIVE
Irritating material	DANGEROUS

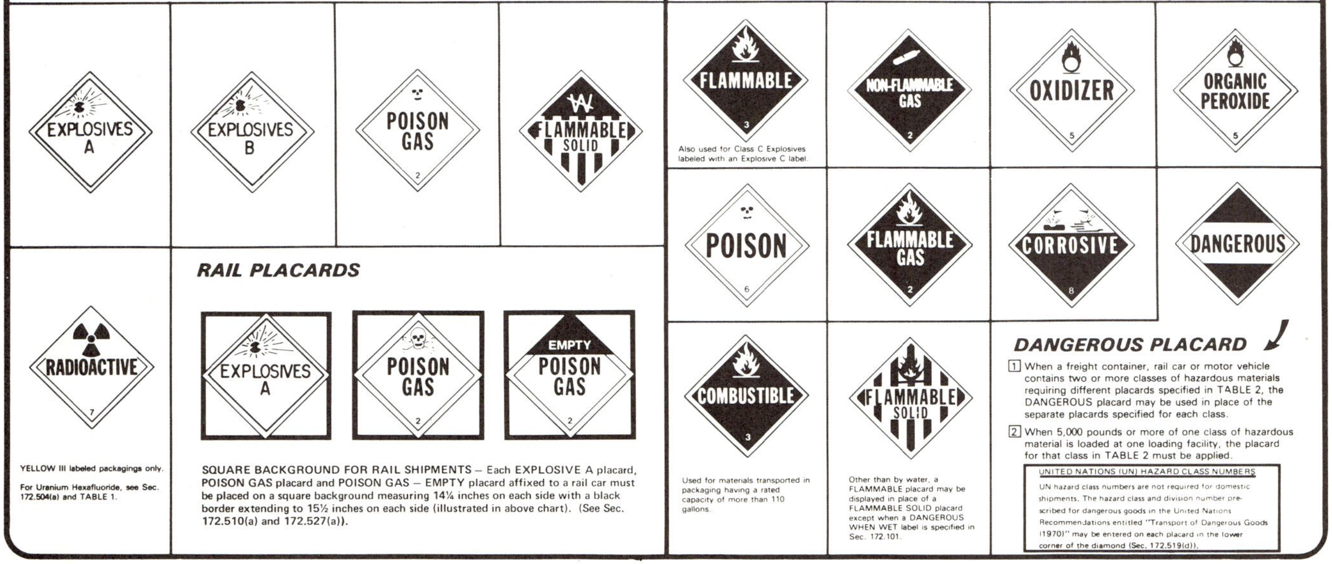

FLAMMABLE 3

Also used for Class C Explosives labeled with an Explosive C label.

NON-FLAMMABLE GAS 2

OXIDIZER 5

ORGANIC PEROXIDE 5

POISON 6

FLAMMABLE GAS 2

CORROSIVE 8

DANGEROUS

COMBUSTIBLE 3

Used for materials transported in packaging having a rated capacity of more than 110 gallons.

FLAMMABLE SOLID

Other than by water, a FLAMMABLE placard may be displayed in place of a FLAMMABLE SOLID placard except when a DANGEROUS WHEN WET label is specified in Sec. 172.101.

DANGEROUS PLACARD

1. When a freight container, rail car or motor vehicle contains two or more classes of hazardous materials requiring different placards specified in TABLE 2, the DANGEROUS placard may be used in place of the separate placards specified for each class.
2. When 5,000 pounds or more of one class of hazardous material is loaded at one loading facility, the placard for that class in TABLE 2 must be applied.

UNITED NATIONS (UN) HAZARD CLASS NUMBERS

UN hazard class numbers are not required for domestic shipments. The hazard class and division number prescribed for dangerous goods in the United Nations Recommendations entitled "Transport of Dangerous Goods (1970)" may be entered on each placard in the lower corner of the diamond (Sec. 172.519(d)).

Fig. 10-2 A DOT (U.S. Department of Transportation) display of warning placards.

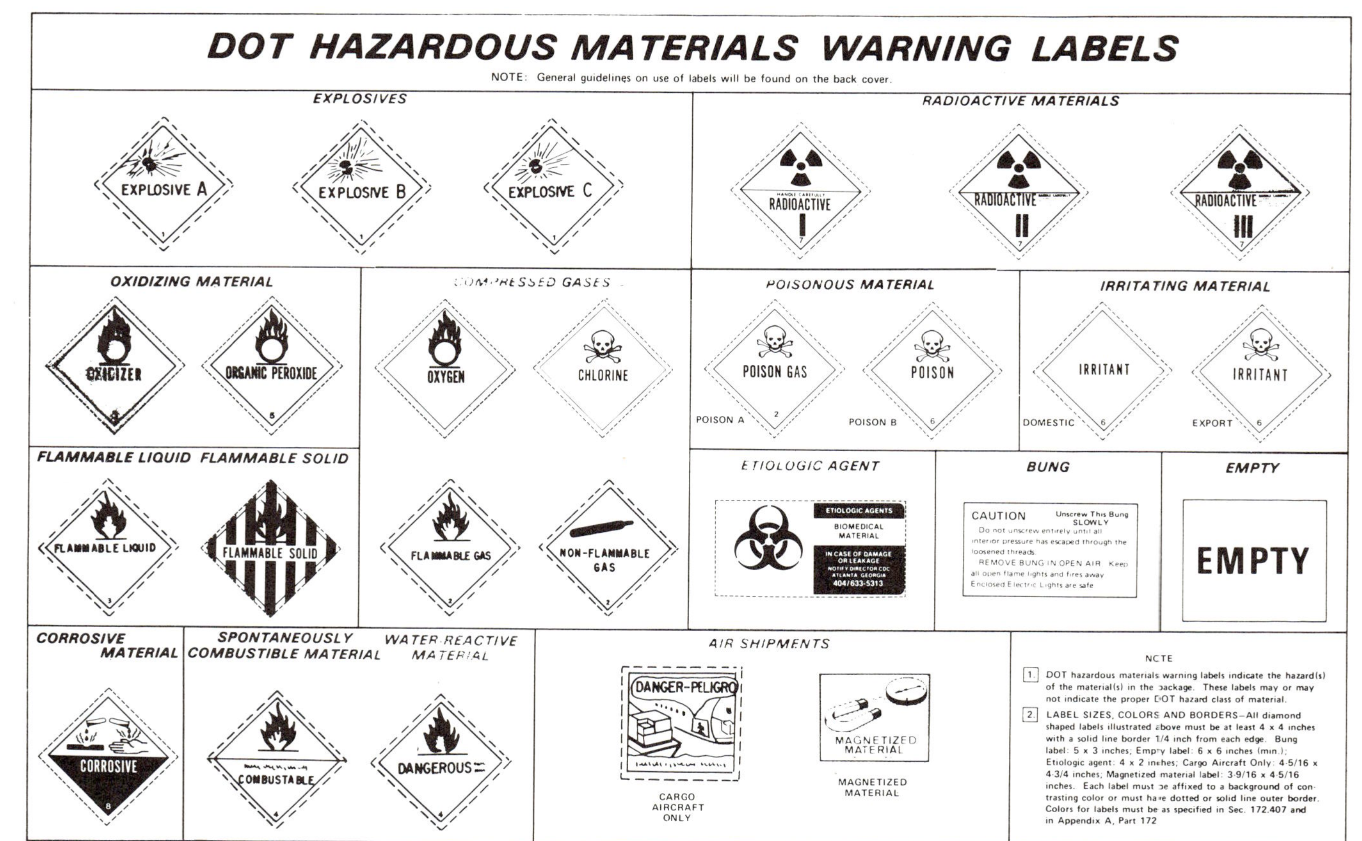

Fig. 10-3 A DOT materials labeling system.

able for the thousands who need training so badly. Also, the training too often is simply offered, and the trainee's retention is not measured. Testing programs during or subsequent to the teaching effort are simply not adequate. To issue a certificate of training without some form of testing is not realistic and of course reflects on our overall national effectiveness. The other shortfall in this area of training is publicity. The author made a significant effort to locate and list the training available, yet the list is meager. Undoubtedly, there are courses available that are not listed. Doesn't that fact alone indicate the nation's need to formalize the training effort?

10-3 RECOGNITION TRAINING AND PRACTICE

Airline baggage handlers, bus drivers, truck drivers, railroad personnel, facility operations personnel—anyone who could become even remotely involved with chemicals—should undergo recognition training. *The U.S. Department of Transportation,* Research and Special Programs Administration, Materials Transportation Bureau, Washington, DC 20590, publishes a free package of material titled "Hazardous Materials Transportation." Included in this package are numerous valuable documents such as a pamphlet on "How to Use the Department of Transportation's Hazardous Material Regulations" and charts showing both DOT warning placards and warning labels (see Figures 10-2 and 10-3). The importance of becoming familiar with this data cannot be overemphasized. Hazardous materials ready for transportation (in drums, cargo tanks, rail cars, etc.) must be labeled or placarded as a matter of law. You must be able to recognize them. Recognition training must be accompanied with the warning, however, that no label, placard, or marking should be casually trusted.

Another vital part of basic instruction should involve the concept of first-sight–first-smell training. Many dangerous chemicals have easily recognized odors, and many have visible characteristics that pertain to groupings such as organophosphates, acids, chlorinated hydrocarbons, and corrosives. That first smell and your strong legs may some day save your life. All of this kind of training should focus on defensive withdrawal reactions; your job doesn't require a total understanding of the chemical or chemicals involved.

Finally, the bottom line will always be practice. It doesn't matter whose time is involved—yours or the company's. Take an hour from time to time and refresh yourself. Every day there are literally thousands of people—driving, loading, filling, or otherwise dealing with chemicals—who have no idea what they are handling.

STOP-PRESS ADDENDUM TO CHAPTER 9

The following information was received too late to incorporate it into Chapter 9, but the author feels that it is important enough to be included in this part of the book, albeit out of sequence.

9-2A TECHNICAL INFORMATION SERVICE

The American Chemical Society has a Health and Safety Referral Service, available unfortunately, only during business hours. Call (202)872-4511.

9-5A REFERENCE BOOKS AND GUIDES

1 *Management of Uncontrolled Hazardous Waste Sites,* USEPA National Conference on Waste Sites, Oct. 15–17, 1980 (LC 80-83-541), Hazardous Materials Control Institute, Silver Spring, MD 20190.

2 Zajic, J.E., and W.A. Himmelman: *Highly Hazardous Material Spills and Emergency Planning,* Marcel Dekker, New York, 1978.

3 *Journal of Hazardous Materials,* a new quarterly, is published by Elsevier North-Holland in Amsterdam; for information, write to the American affiliate at 52 Vanderbilt Ave., New York, NY 10017.

4 For information about problems involving railroads and other forms of transportation, consult the publications of the National Transportation Safety Board, 800 Independence Ave. SW, Washington, DC 20591.

5 Fawcett, H.H., and W.S. Wood (eds.): *Safety and Health in Chemical Operations,* 2d ed., Wiley-Interscience, New York, 1981.

6 Ember, L.R. Uncertain Science Pushes Love Canal Solutions to Political, Legal Arenas, *Chemical and Engineering News,* Vol 58, No. 32, August 11, 1980, pages 22–29.

part
FOUR

Public Information

chapter

ELEVEN

Hazardous Spills and the Media

The public must be kept informed of all phases of a hazardous substance accident—the actual event, the results, and on-scene cleanup activities. The media are the only means by which this can be done. Radio, television, and the press have a duty to disseminate news of such events to the public in a timely and accurate manner. No official at any level has a right to shape the news, to attempt to downplay the scope of the event, or to restrain the media for reasons other than safety. In fact the same duty that applies to the media applies to the on-scene official. The federal government takes a strong and clear stand on public information. In Chapter 2 we quoted a brief statement on this position from the 1510 plan. State sunshine laws, if not explicit in defining public information exercises, certainly imply that the public should be kept informed at all times. Who can cite even one justification for the local official not keeping his or her people totally informed?

But public information has even a broader meaning in the context of accidents. Pre-event information is as vital a part of the whole exercise as is postevent information. It is not enough that we perfect the art of publishing information about accidents; we should work toward a goal of proliferation of news and media information alerting the public to governmental preparedness for any kind of disaster.

11-1 WHO SHOULD HANDLE THE MEDIA?

No single situation can destroy a well-run exercise quicker than dissension among officials over who should be speaking to the press. This is not really a matter of personalities, as we frequently hear; the problem arises from practical duty pressures. Consider the fact that the federal, state, and local on-scene coordinators must be available to the media. The issues at the level each represents are *that* different. The public is interested in all issues, and it is the job of the media to look for and report them. The spillor is also a target for questions and has a duty to speak. It would be ideal if only one person represented all people to the press, but that would never work; it never has. There are questions that you simply cannot answer because they are either outside of your agency's scope or, as a matter of pure logistics, you simply do not know the answers.

Basically, media people are fair. They want the simple, straightforward truth, but if you lead with your chin they will quote you. There are a number of things media representatives want and need, and they will persist until they get all or at least some of them:

1 They want to speak to decision makers. Spills are dynamic and are not well described by scheduled press releases.

2 They want to speak to people on scene. If you are a state, local, or federal official in a remote location, do not expect the media to call you for details. The worst thing you can do is to send a person on scene with obvious authority but with instructions that all press statements must come from you.

3 For color, the media are always interested in off-the-cuff remarks. "Hip shooters" seem to get into trouble quickly.

4 They want to see the wreck, fire, or whatever, and they want pictures. If safety permits, you should make a reasonable effort to accommodate them.

Who is going to handle all of this? How can we resolve the issue of who speaks to the media? There are three major groupings that have a responsibility to respond to media questions: government, scientific or specialty personnel, and the spillor.

Government

Federal

At a spill emergency, all *pollution-oriented* statements by federal officials will be made through the federal news center on-scene. Any agency on the RRT is entitled to representation on the news team, and officials of the various agencies are encouraged to discuss their specialty areas with the media at the numerous news conferences. The federal news team will be headed by a professional press representative from the OSC's agency unless the chairman of the RRT or the OSC directs otherwise. All federal officials, including the OSC, should avoid individual contacts with the media. Federal agencies with independent authority such as the National Transportation Safety Board will conduct their own press conferences, hearings, etc.

State

Most states will want consolidated news releases. Some have predesigned news teams that respond like those of the federal government. As a suggestion, the state would benefit substantially by having its representative or representatives participate in the federal conferences, and for convenience sake they may want to be included as a member of a federal–state news team housed in the OSC's command post.

Local

Local governments also need consolidated news releases. The suggestion is the same: Have representatives on a federal–state–local news team. The press is keenly interested in your view, and it is doubtful that you will be overshadowed by federal and state officials.

Scientific and Specialty Personnel

Most technical and scientific information should be channeled through the composite federal, state, and local news team discussed above. If there is a hot issue, be at the news conference; you will certainly be asked questions. There are occasions when specialty personnel will be quizzed about topics that only they can discuss, such as how the biorespirator works, where the ambulance picked up the last victim, etc. This is unavoidable and is part of the news spectrum. Questions involving scientific speculation, estimation of injury, quantification of damages, and reoccupation timing, however, are best left to the entire news team.

Spillor

Your liabilities are as critical to you as your public image; certainly you need a single news contact for the media. You may wish to participate on the composite news team which affords the media an opportunity to quiz everyone in one session, eliminates many conflicting statements, and saves everyone's time. No one is going to dominate news conferences of this kind; the media are aware of those present and what they can contribute. Figure 11-1 shows a composite news team press conference in session.

Fig. 11-1 Composite news-team press conference at the command post, Crestview, Florida, 1979.

11-2 WHAT KIND OF INFORMATION WILL THE MEDIA SEEK?

The questions asked by the media vary with the accident, but they largely relate to the interests of the general public. Among these questions, the media do seem to have favorites:

Who was at fault?

How much was spilled?

What is the damage?

Who is in charge?

Will legal actions be taken? By whom?

Questions of costs: How much? Who is responsible for?

Mr. X said there was vandalism; do you agree?

Mrs. Y said there is no pollution; is that true?

Dr. Z at Cobalt University says this chemical is harmless; is it?

Is there a chance of more fire or explosion?

How many were injured?

Has there really been trouble at the roadblock?

Mr. X said the area evacuated is adequate; do you agree?

Would you say there will be a large fish kill?

When will the water-treatment plant be back in operation?

Your district office in Cobalt says there will be no adverse health effects; is that correct?

Why can't industry prevent this?

Doesn't this stuff cause cancer?

You can see here the basic style, the probing questions, the questions that may go beyond your knowledge or field of expertise, and the questions seeking verification or disagreement. If you take a closer look, however, it is obvious that all of these questions can be fielded by a composite news team.

11-3 SOME DOS AND DON'TS AT THE SCENE

Dos

1 Accommodate the media as much as possible; make the news available to them.

2 Schedule news conferences and avoid written releases.

3 Be direct and specific.

4 Always, *always* tell the truth; don't hedge.

5 Hold public hearings at least twice during a week-long event and invite the press.

6 Have news conferences immediately after any meeting from which you barred the media or public. (See number 11 under *Don'ts*)

7 Decide immediately, or have it stated in your plan, who is going to represent you to the media. Stick with him or her.

8 Send a press representative to the OSC's command post.

9 Be sure you are in contact at all times with the OSC's command post.

Don'ts

1 Don't argue with each other in front of the press. State your dissenting opinion; it will be noted.

2 Avoid giving gut opinions or conjecturing.

3 Don't be evasive. If you don't know, say so, or refer the question to someone who does.

4 Don't be critical in a personal manner; e.g., avoid personal remarks about other people on-scene.

5 Don't be philosophical. These kinds of discussions are extremely susceptible to being quoted out of context.

6 Don't make off-the-record comments. You may see them in print—and retractions are buried on the back pages.

7 Avoid friendly chats with media people. They are professionals, and your casual comments may appear in print.

8 Avoid bad language; it is good color to the news person.

9 Don't hide from the media. They can sense this and form an unfavorable opinion of you as a credible source of news.

10 Don't field questions that are beyond your knowledge or expertise.

11 Do not allow media persons to attend your RRT meetings. These are *technical* meetings. They will always be lively discussions and can last forever if people are performing rather than dealing with the problem. Also avoid having the public at these meetings.

12 Avoid holding RRT meetings outdoors. Anyone can drift in, hear a discussion on priorities, and draw the wrong conclusions.

13 Don't be hostile toward the media; there is no sense in that.

11-5 HOME-OFFICE NEWS ACTIVITIES

Everyone on-scene has a home office of some kind. The people located in these offices must be kept informed at all times; after all, they get calls from higher offices. *Everyone* wants to know what is going on.

Most agencies have a professional public information staff. To avoid confusion and tying up very limited phone lines, the various members of the composite news team should call their respective offices at least twice a day. The news can then filter upward. Once again this is an endorsement of the composite news-team concept. With everyone working in close proximity, there is little chance of strange, false, or exaggerated stories getting out.

Finally, the home office must *never* release information that is not cleared by their on-scene representative.

Index